DAVID

Anchoring Your Heart
Close to God

BACK TO THE BIBLE
Publishing

DAVID: ANCHORING YOUR HEART CLOSE TO GOD

BACK TO THE BIBLE PUBLISHING
P.O. Box 82808
Lincoln, NE 68501

Editors: Rachel Derowitsch, Allen Bean
Cover and interior design: Robert Greuter & Associates
Art and editorial direction: Kim Johnson

For information about language translations, international availability, and licensing for non-English publication, contact Back to the Bible Publishing at the above address.

Additional copies of this book are available from Back to the Bible Publishing. You may order by calling 1-800-759-2425 or through our Web site at www.resources.backtothebible.org.

1 2 3 4 5 6 7 8 9 10 – 05 04 03 02 01 00

ISBN 0-8474-0203-7

Printed in the USA

CONTENTS

$\mathcal{W}$elcome to our Bible study time together!

Meet Your Bible Study Leaders

Dr. Gene A. Getz is a pastor, church planter, seminary professor, and author of nearly 50 books, including *The Measure of a Man* and the popular *Men of Character* series. Presently, Gene serves as senior pastor at Fellowship Bible Church North in Plano, Texas, and is director of the Center for Church Renewal. He is also host of the syndicated radio program *Renewal*.

Dr. Tony Beckett is the Associate Bible Teacher for the international ministry Back to the Bible. He has pastored churches in Iowa, Ohio, and Pennsylvania, worked with camp ministries and church leadership councils, and served as an area representative for Baseball Chapel. Dr. Beckett and his wife, Joan, have three daughters.

This study on the life of David is another in the *Interacting with God* series. It is our hope and prayer that this approach to Bible study will help you apply God's Word to your daily life.

The *Interacting with God* study guide is intended to do more than teach you basic facts. You still need to know, however, what the Bible says. In order to help with that learning process, each lesson is centered on an event from the life of David. You will learn names, places, and events, all of which are Bible facts that you should know.

Beyond learning what the Bible says, however, you also need to learn what it means for your life today. Woven throughout each lesson are questions to help you do that. These are "interactive" questions written to help you interact with God.

Interacting with God is essentially thinking through what a Scripture passage means for you today. You listen to or read the text, learn what it says, and then think through how to incorporate its truths in your life every day. If you are working through this guide with a group, you will not only think through but also talk through the meaning of each lesson. The Introduction to Interacting with God will help you understand how to best use this study guide.

In Deuteronomy 31:12 Moses instructed the people to "listen and learn to fear the LORD . . . and follow carefully all the words of [the] law." The sequence in this verse is vital! *Listen.* We must first of all be hearers of God's Word. *Learn.* We must do more than just read or hear the words of Scripture. The lessons it contains must be stored in our memory. *Live.* We must put to use (follow) in our daily lives what we learn.

Listen, learn, and live are all vital elements, but they must be kept in that sequence. Application comes after learning. Learning is the result of listening. Start with listening to what the Bible says, learn its truths, and apply them to your life today.

It is our prayer that this Bible study tool will help you explore the Scriptures and respond to God as you develop your personal relationship with Him. We pray that you will experience God's best as you grow more intimate with Him and discover the joy of being a part of a healthy Body of Christ—your church.

Gene A. Getz

Tony Beckett

Introduction to Interacting with God

Even if you have already studied another *Interacting with God* Bible study workbook, you may want to review the following material. These pages are intended to help you get the most out of your study.

Personal and Small-Group Bible Study

This workbook is one course in a series of Bible study tools developed to help Christians experience a dynamic relationship with God. New courses in this series will be released regularly to help you accomplish two primary goals:

1. To know and understand what God is saying to you in the Bible text studied, bringing you to a deeper, more intimate love relationship with Him.

2. Together with other Christians, to grow in your love for one another and increasingly become a healthy and mature Body of Christ that brings glory to God.

Those goals may sound too high or unattainable to you. Indeed, we're not able to accomplish them in our human abilities. Only God can lead His people in such a way that these two goals can be accomplished in your life and in your church. That's why we will be pointing you through the Bible to the Lord and your relationship with Him. As you interact with Him and His Word, the Holy Spirit will guide you and your group to experience God's best. The coming weeks will be a spiritual adventure as God opens your minds to understand and apply His Word to your life, your family, your church, your community, and your world.

If you're not a Christian, don't stop now. We want to help you come to know more about God, so stay with us. This study will help you understand the kind of love relationship God desires to have with you. We will occasionally ask you to examine your relationship with God, knowing that He will be working in your life to reveal Himself and draw you to His Son, Jesus Christ. Being in a small group with other Christians will give you a chance to see up close the difference God makes in a life.

This *Interacting with God* course can be used as either a personal or group Bible study guide. In this introduction we've included suggestions for using this study, but the material is flexible, so you can adapt it to your situation.

The six lessons can be covered in six sessions. We suggest that you (and your group) adopt a pace with which you are comfortable. If some lessons need more time than one group meeting, please allow for that. It may be that at times during the study, the Holy Spirit will lead you to slow down and even dwell on a point of significant impact for you or those with whom you are studying.

Self-Paced Bible Study

Each lesson has been divided into four parts so you can study it over a period of several days. Since each part includes a study of God's Word and a time for prayer and interacting with God, you may want to use this as your daily devotional guide. The Bible study has several features.

Scripture Reading. In Part 1 of each lesson, you'll be given an assignment to read or listen to a portion of Scripture. There may be more than one passage listed. It is best to begin your study with reading the key passages listed there. When studying the Bible, the best place to begin is with reading the Bible! That seems simple enough, but at times people read about the Bible rather than read the Bible itself. Start with the text and then proceed to the lesson itself. Audio versions of the Bible are available at Christian bookstores. You might prefer listening to the passage being read. You might even want to listen to it several times during the course while driving in your car or at some other time. We encourage you to read or listen to all of 1 and 2 Samuel.

Throughout the workbook, key texts and, at times, entire passages are provided for you to read. This is to save you time in your study. We know many people don't take time to look up Bible verses that are only referenced. We want you to read God's Word because God uses it to speak to you. The Bible verses are the most important words in this book. As you read verses that are especially meaningful to you, you may want to turn to them in your Bible and underline them for future reference.

Interactives. Woven throughout the lessons are questions and statements intended to help you interact with God. The purpose of these questions is to help you apply the Word of God to your life today. These questions are marked with an arrow ▶. Some will be discussion questions that you can use with a small group. Others will be very personal, not intended for sharing in an open group. There may not be an obvious answer to the question, either. At times you will be instructed to read a section aloud, and at other times you will be encouraged to pause right then to pray 🖐.

Use these interactives to help you take what you have learned and apply it to your life. That is one of the unique strengths of this approach to Bible study. It helps you learn the lesson and think through how to live it. If you just read through this material and don't take time to interact with God, the information will be of little help to you. We don't want you just to know about God; we want you to experience Him in a dynamic and personal relationship. Do not neglect the times for prayer, both as an individual and in a small group. Spending time with Him in prayer will be a key part of your experience.

Life Applications. Occasionally you will notice in the margin an arrow like this one ▶. It is there to draw your attention to a special point. God has given us His Word not just to increase our knowledge but to change our lives. These arrows are placed by paragraphs that have special application to your life today.

Main Column and Margin. The primary column for your study is the wide one on the right side of each page. Always start reading and studying in that column. Read through the lesson. It is a good practice to read with a highlighter pen to mark key words, phrases, or sentences.

The left margin will be a place for references. Key texts will be listed there. Occasionally we'll place an important statement or illustration in the margin.

Small-Group Bible Study

A Christian who was a part of the early church in Jerusalem would have had both large-group and small-group experiences. Both Acts 2 and 5 refer to the fact that the believers met together in the temple courts and from house to house.

"Every day they continued to meet together in the temple courts. They broke bread in their homes and ate together with glad and sincere hearts, praising God and enjoying the favor of all the people. And the Lord added to their number daily those who were being saved" (Acts 2:46–47).

"Day after day, in the temple courts and from house to house, they never stopped teaching and proclaiming the good news that Jesus is the Christ" (Acts 5:42).

Worship services in a local church today are large-group experiences like the early church had in the temple courts. The early church's small-group experiences took place in homes.

Today, many people are involved in small groups for study of the Word and building relationships with other believers.

Small groups may be called a variety of names and may be structured in a variety of ways. A list of small group opportunities includes, but is not limited to, Sunday school class, discipleship class, home Bible study group, cell group, midweek Bible study, and men's or women's ministry group.

This study guide is designed to be flexible enough that an individual or study group can use it. It would even work well as a tool for family devotions.

The following are some suggestions for using this guide effectively in a small group.

Leadership. We recommend that each group have a leader and, if possible, a leader apprentice or coleader. The apprentice is learning how to lead and is available to fill in if the leader is unable to attend a meeting. A coleader could be an apprentice or could be another individual who shares the leadership of the group or is the substitute leader when needed.

A leader does not have to be a content expert. Nor does a leader need to have studied through the entire workbook before beginning to lead, either. All members will study the content of this workbook in preparation for the meetings.

Group Size. Since the purpose of the small group is to allow for close relationships between believers, the group can't grow too large without hindering spiritual intimacy. A group that reaches 16-20 in regular attendance is probably ready to multiply.

Leading a Small-Group Meeting

The following suggestions will help the leaders of a small-group Bible study.

Plan how you will use your time. People appreciate knowing that their time will be used wisely, so set in advance your basic schedule. It may be that you will begin with refreshments,

move to the study, and conclude with prayer. Some prefer to start the study time first and then allow for refreshments and extended fellowship time after. The Small-Group Meeting guide at the end of each lesson will help you progress through the lesson as a group. It goes through the same basic steps each week, though you can deviate from it to meet the needs of your group.

Work at building relationships. One of the joys of being a disciple is fellowship with others. Be sure that all members are introduced by name to the group. Any visitors or new members should be welcomed. Sharing some basic information, such as place of employment or special interests, can help people get to know one another.

Commit to the small group. Some people find it a special blessing or benefit to have a formal group covenant. One is included in this book. It is a way of saying, "Count on me." It also means that the group is saying, "We will be there for you." If someone is missing, make contact with him or her. Do not assume the reason for the absence. You may be able to help with a problem that kept that person from attending. Also, you may become aware of a need. Perhaps God will enable the group to minister to that person at that time.

How to Use the Small-Group Meeting Guides

At the end of each chapter you will find a page to assist the leader(s) of the group. It outlines the basic format for each small-group meeting. Feel free to adjust the format to best fit your group. If you need to take more than one session together to work on a lesson, then allow the extra time. Do not rush just to complete the book in six weeks. Take the time needed to learn the lessons God has for you.

The first two activities in the meeting guides are fellowship-oriented. Begin with prayer and then work on building your relationships with one another.

The Reviewing the Lesson section is important. It will help you go back through the text of this workbook. It is vital for each member of the group to have the account from the Bible clearly in mind. While we are eager to see how the lesson applies to our lives, we must begin with the Word. Once that is clearly in mind, we can then move on to application.

The next part of the guide is Applying the Truths to Life. This is where the leader is most involved in shaping the time with the group. Look over the interactive questions. Time will probably not allow for your group to discuss all of them. Encourage the group members to work through all the interactives during the week. Then, during your time together, choose ones you think are most appropriate to discuss together.

Finally, use your time together to build fellowship and reach out to others. Specific suggestions are given in each lesson for activities that will enable this. Sharing refreshments at the beginning or end of your meeting can aid in the building of relationships. Encourage everyone to contribute in this aspect of your group fellowship. This will help keep the provision and preparation of food from being a burden to one and allow every member to feel that they have a part in the group.

Back to the Bible Resources

Back to the Bible began in 1939 primarily as a radio Bible-teaching ministry. To continue leading people into a dynamic relationship with God, the ministry has expanded to include the publication of resources for use with small groups. These small-group Bible studies are being developed as a service to the local church to help you experience the full dimensions of being a healthy Body of Christ.

Workbooks should be available through your local Christian bookstores. Any bookstore, however, can carry them. If you don't have a Christian bookstore, work with a local bookseller to stock the books for you and other Christians in your area. They can use the ISBN information on the back of this workbook to order them. If they should have difficulty, encourage them to contact Back to the Bible Publishing at 1-888-559-7878. Since you will need larger-than-normal quantities, place your order several weeks in advance of your planned starting time. If you prefer, you may order directly from Back to the Bible by calling 1-800-759-2425 or by visiting our Web site (www.resources.backtothebible.org). There you also can learn about other available resources and of new products to be released soon.

The Man Who Lost a Crown
A Renewed Heart

1 Samuel 16

Imagine the following advertisement in the classifieds section of the newspaper. "Help wanted: Position opening soon for a king to succeed sometimes popular and sometimes successful one-generation monarchy. Don't call us; we'll call you."

The ad would point to a position presently filled but soon to be vacant. It also would communicate that the current king was not always popular nor entirely successful. It would indicate that something had gone awry, because monarchies usually last longer than one generation. The last line would say that it is a position into which one is placed, not a position for which one applies.

Vacancy, king needed, God to do the selecting. The man who has the job is about to lose it.

While those exact words are not found in the Bible, that is essentially the message delivered by the prophet Samuel to King Saul in 1 Samuel 13:13–14: "'You acted foolishly,' Samuel said. 'You have not kept the command the LORD your God gave you; if you had, he would have established your kingdom over Israel for all time. But now your kingdom will not endure; the LORD has sought out a man after his own heart and appointed him leader of his people, because you have not kept the LORD's command.'"

One of the greatest challenges every Christian faces is to keep his spiritual, ethical, and moral bearings during his journey through life. Saul had failed to do that. Prominence and success went to his head, which always affects the heart—the area where we are all vulnerable.

In contrast there is David, who is described in 1 Samuel 13:14 as a man after God's own heart. David had his failures, but what set him apart was his heart.

Our desire should be to anchor our hearts close to God. David's example helps us do that. David illustrates the heart each of us needs both in times of success and times of failure. By looking at his heart we learn lessons to apply to our own hearts. As we live out these lessons, our hearts will be anchored closer to God.

These studies focus on David's heart and what it was like. In this first lesson we will see the importance of a renewed heart. Our attention will be drawn first to Saul, the man whose heart was changed by God (1 Sam. 10:9–10). When God equipped Saul to be king, He began in the heart. Sadly, Saul failed. As the Bible tells of the conclusion of Saul's reign, it then draws our attention to David. The contrast is remarkable and reminds us of the importance of having a heart for God.

▶ **1. Sometimes people speak of the need for a moral compass. Which of the following do people use today to guide them in their decision making? Add to the list ones that come to your mind.**

☐ philosophy   ☐ feelings   ☐ astrology   ☐ the Bible

☐ others _____

▶ **2. Included in the above list is the Bible. How do people make God's Word their moral compass?**

• read it   • attend church   • learn the lessons found in it

• memorize verses   • look for practical application

Which of these ways is most significant to you? In what other ways do you learn what the Bible teaches?

_____

_____

PART 1: Interacting with the Scripture

Reading/Hearing God's Word

▶ **3. Using your Bible, read or listen to the passages of Scripture listed in the margin. As you begin, ask God to speak to you through His Word. Watch for verses or ideas that are especially meaningful to you today. Once you finish reading, check the box indicating the passage(s) you read.**

Meditating on God's Word

▶ **4. Write a brief summary of a meaningful verse or idea you noticed.**

_____

_____

_____

Read or Listen to:

☐ 1 Samuel 13:1–15

☐ 1 Samuel 15

☐ 1 Samuel 16

☐ Psalm 24

1 Samuel 16:7–13

"But the LORD said to Samuel, 'Do not consider his appearance or his height, for I have rejected him. The LORD does not look at the things man looks at. Man looks at the outward appearance, but the LORD looks at the heart.'

"Then Jesse called Abinadab and had him pass in front of Samuel. But Samuel said, 'The LORD has not chosen this one either.' Jesse then had Shammah pass by, but Samuel said, 'Nor has the LORD chosen this one.' Jesse had seven of his sons pass before Samuel, but Samuel said to him, 'The LORD has not chosen these.' So he asked Jesse, 'Are these all the sons you have?'

"'There is still the youngest,' Jesse answered, 'but he is tending the sheep.' Samuel said, 'Send for him; we will not sit down until he arrives.'

"So he sent and had him brought in. He was ruddy, with a fine appearance and handsome features.

"Then the LORD said, 'Rise and anoint him; he is the one.'

"So Samuel took the horn of oil and anointed him in the presence of his brothers, and from that day on the Spirit of the LORD came upon David in power. Samuel then went to Ramah."

Understanding God's Word

▶ 5. Read again the focal passage for this week's lesson (1 Sam. 16:7–13) in the margin. Underline any key phrases or ideas that seem especially meaningful to you.

▶ 6. Look back at these verses. Circle one of the underlined phrases or words that you would like to understand or experience more fully.

Looking through the Scripture to God

Now pause to pray. Pray that:

• God will use His Word in your heart.

• God's Spirit will guide your study.

• the work of God's Son will be understood.

• you will know that your heart is renewed.

PART 2: Saul Readied to Be King

Life is filled with contrasts. Some are good and some are bad—a contrast in itself. Some happen quickly, such as a tranquil environment suddenly rocked by an earthquake. Some happen gradually, as when the sun sets, transforming our part of the earth from light to darkness, or when an illness slowly take its toll and eventually leaves strong, healthy people weak and sickly. Some are concurrent experiences, such as eating sweet-and-sour food or enduring the pain and joy of childbirth.

Contrasts and incongruities are a part of life. That's why humans have used contrast as a literary technique ever since we began expressing reality—as well as fiction—in writing.

Biblical writers, inspired by the Holy Spirit, also used this literary technique. The author of 1 Samuel used a startling contrast that should turn our heads every time we read it. When Samuel anointed David to be the second king of Israel, we read these statements:

"The Spirit of the LORD came upon David in power" (1 Sam. 16:13).

"Now the Spirit of the LORD had departed from Saul" (v. 14).

In Old Testament times, the Spirit was given to specific individuals selected for special tasks. Saul was one such person. God did not just anoint him king and let him rule in his own strength. Instead, He specifically worked in Saul's heart and life. He prepared him to be king in three ways.

God's worker prepared Saul.

The prophet Samuel anointed Saul (see 1 Sam. 10:1 in the margin). This was a sign of God's selection. Samuel was also there both to influence Saul and to be involved in the affairs of the country. Saul truly was blessed to have Samuel. Sadly, there is no indication that Saul recognized the value of what God had given to him in the prophet.

▶ 7. Read Ephesians 4:16–17 in the margin. God has given special workers to equip His people today. Name the individuals who are equipping you. _____

_____

How does God want you to respond to these people?

☐ learn from   ☐ listen to   ☐ esteem highly

☐ submit to   ☐ share with   ☐ encourage

☐ other _____

God's word prepared Saul.

God revealed himself to Samuel through His word according to 1 Samuel 3:21. The next verse then states that "Samuel's word came to all Israel" (4:1). He served Israel as prophet, priest, and judge. He was not only God's worker but also one who spoke God's words.

Samuel had spent all night talking with Saul (9:25–27). As they prepared to leave, he said to Saul, "Tell the servant to go on ahead of us . . . but you stay here awhile, so that I may give you a message from God." The message was that the Lord had anointed Saul "leader over his inheritance" (10:1).

God's worker gave Saul God's word to prepare him to be king.

▶ 8. We have God's written Word, the Bible. How often do you read it?

☐ daily   ☐ twice or more weekly   ☐ weekly

☐ monthly   ☐ seldom   ☐ only in church services

☐ never

Do you have a regular reading plan?

☐ yes   ☐ no

---

1 Samuel 10:1

"Then Samuel took a flask of oil and poured it on Saul's head and kissed him, saying, 'Has not the LORD anointed you leader over his inheritance?'"

Ephesians 4:16–17

"From him [Christ] the whole body, joined and held together by every supporting ligament, grows and builds itself up in love, as each part does its work.

"So I tell you this, and insist on it in the Lord, that you must no longer live as the Gentiles do, in the futility of their thinking."

Before continuing in this study, make a written commitment to read the Bible regularly and frequently. _____

_____

_____

God's work in his life prepared Saul.

One unusual way God worked in Saul's life was through animals. Saul first met Samuel when he was trying to find his father's donkeys. They were lost, but only as long as God wanted them lost. God used the donkeys to bring Saul to see the prophet. When Saul went to see Samuel about the animals, he was told, "Do not worry about them; they have been found" (1 Sam. 9:20). This news came right after Samuel said, "Today you are to eat with me, and in the morning I will let you go and will tell you all that is in your heart" (v. 19).

Another way God worked in Saul's life was with the offering that was shared with him (read 1 Sam. 10:3–4 in the margin).

1 Samuel 10:3–4

"'Then you will go on from there until you reach the great tree of Tabor. Three men going up to God at Bethel will meet you there. One will be carrying three young goats, another three loaves of bread, and another a skin of wine. They will greet you and offer you two loaves of bread, which you will accept from them.'"

▶ **9. Describe in your own words what happened in these verses and how it was a work of God in Saul's life.** _____

_____

_____

_____

Compare what you have written with the following answers.

- It was the fulfillment of a sign.

- It was an unmistakable confirmation of God's work.

- God was bringing together events to convince Saul that he was to be the king.

▶ **10. What does God use today to show us His will? (Be careful here. The temptation is to be very subjective.)**

_____

_____

_____

Compare what you have written with the following answers.

- He uses His Word.

- He uses His Spirit.

- He uses godly counselors.

In addition, Samuel told Saul that on his way to Gibeah he would meet a procession of prophets. The Spirit of the Lord would come upon him and he would prophesy with them. Then Samuel added, "And you will be changed into a different person" (1 Sam. 10:6).

There are a number of examples in the Old Testament of the Spirit of God coming upon men. God sovereignly selected them for special tasks, and often they were enabled to prophesy and speak God's words to the children of Israel.

For instance, the Lord selected Bezalel to take responsibility to build the tabernacle in the wilderness. To help him achieve this incredible feat, the Lord anointed Bezalel in a special way with His Spirit. Communicating directly with Moses, God said, "I have filled him with the Spirit of God, with skill, ability and knowledge in all kinds of crafts—to make artistic designs for work in gold, silver and bronze, to cut and set stones, to work in wood, and to engage in all kinds of craftsmanship" (Ex. 31:3–5).

Moses also experienced God's special anointing. On one occasion, when he was terribly discouraged with what appeared to be an impossible task, God anointed 70 other men to help Moses lead the children of Israel through the wilderness:

> The LORD said to Moses: "Bring me seventy of Israel's elders who are known to you as leaders and officials among the people. Have them come to the Tent of Meeting, that they may stand there with you. I will come down and speak with you there, and I will take of the Spirit that is on you and put the Spirit on them. They will help you carry the burden of the people so that you will not have to carry it alone" (Num. 11:16–17).

We can find a number of other illustrations of this Old Testament phenomenon.

▶ **11. Read the following verses and note what is said about the Spirit of the Lord coming upon these individuals.**

• Balaam (Num. 24:2) _____

• Joshua (Num. 27:18; Deut. 34:9) _____

• Othniel (Judges 3:10) _____

• Gideon (Judges 6:34) _____

• Jephthah (Judges 11:29) _____

• Samson (Judges 14:6, 19; 15:14) _____

In each instance, the Spirit of the Lord came upon these men, giving them supernatural abilities.

1 Samuel 10:9

"As Saul turned to leave Samuel, God changed Saul's heart, and all these signs were fulfilled that day."

Acts 1:14

"They all joined together constantly in prayer, along with the women and Mary the mother of Jesus, and with his brothers."

This also happened to Saul when God chose him to be the first king of Israel. We read that "God changed Saul's heart, and . . . the Spirit of God came upon him in power" (1 Sam. 10:9–10), just as the Spirit came upon David the day he was anointed to replace Saul.

All of the examples so far have been of men. But women also were especially selected to serve God. Miriam, Moses' sister, is identified as a "prophetess" (Ex. 15:20). God used her to speak His message to the people of Israel. Another notable woman from the Old Testament was Deborah, whom God chose as a judge in Israel (Judges 4:4).

It is important to note the women who participated in prayer with the men in Acts 1:14 (see margin). The next mention of women, in Peter's sermon, also is significant. He quotes the prophet Joel: "'In the last days, God says, I will pour out my Spirit on all people. Your sons and daughters will prophesy . . . . Even on my servants, both men and women, I will pour out my Spirit'" (Acts 2:17–18). The Holy Spirit is given to all believers, women as well as men.

▶ **12. The New Testament teaches us that God gives spiritual gifts to each of His followers (Rom. 12:6–8; 1 Cor. 12–14). As you think about the work of the Holy Spirit in your life, have you discovered your gift(s)?** _____

What is it/are they? _____

How have you developed that gift(s)? _____

In what way are you using your gift(s) to benefit others in the Body of Christ? _____

_____

What Is the Heart?

In both the Old and New Testaments, the word *heart* refers to the center of an individual's mental, emotional, and spiritual life. It's the "innermost part of man." The heart reflects the real person.

As the *mental center,* the heart knows, understands, reflects, considers, and remembers.

As the *emotional center,* it is the seat of joy, courage, pain, anxiety, despair, sorrow, and fear.

As the *moral center,* the heart is tried, seen, refined, and searched by God.

The Scriptures indicate that a person may have an "evil heart," be "godless in heart," be "perverse and deceitful in heart," and "harden his heart." But a person also can have a "clean heart" and a "new heart."[1]

God fitted Saul for the task of ruling by changing his heart (1 Sam. 10:9). Likewise, when God fits us to serve Him, He starts with the heart. We may have a variety of abilities, but fitness to serve God starts with salvation, which is a matter of the heart.

▶ **13. How and when did you accept Christ as your Savior? Explain to someone else how he also can know that he is saved.**

The importance of a renewed heart is seen in God rejecting Saul.

PART 3: Saul Rejected As King

Saul began his career as a very humble and upright person. But prominence and success soon went to his head, which readily affects the heart—the area where we are all vulnerable. Saul's sinful nature took over and soon dominated his total being, including his actions.

➡ God's work in our life does not leave us without responsibility but rather with increased responsibility.

Saul's failure to be the king God intended led to a series of sad events. First, he demonstrated himself to be self-willed.

▶ **14. Read 1 Samuel 13:11–13 in the margin.**

Saul had been instructed to wait for Samuel to come before attacking the Philistines. Instead, he offered up the burnt offering, something Samuel was supposed to do.

Saul's defense of his actions was based on everything but what he was directly told to do. He said, "When I saw that the men were scattering, and that you [Samuel] did not come . . . , I thought . . . . So I felt compelled to offer the burnt offering." Notice the sequence: I saw . . . I thought . . . I felt. But he disobeyed what God *said*.

The prophet rebuked the king with the words, "You acted foolishly." Had Saul obeyed the Lord, he would have been blessed forever. But from this moment forward, his story is one of psychological, physical, and spiritual deterioration.

1 Samuel 13:11–13

"'What have you done?' asked Samuel.

"Saul replied, 'When I saw that the men were scattering, and that you did not come at the set time, and that the Philistines were assembling at Micmash, I thought, "Now the Philistines will come down against me at Gilgal, and I have not sought the LORD's favor." So I felt compelled to offer the burnt offering.'

"'You acted foolishly,' Samuel said. 'You have not kept the command the LORD your God gave you; if you had, he would have established your kingdom over Israel for all time.'"

▶ **15. Now look at the following passages and write down what Saul did to demonstrate that he was:**

• **Disobedient:** 1 Samuel 15:13–14, 22–23

_____

_____

_____

_____

• **Jealous and hateful:** 1 Samuel 18:8–9; 19:1

_____

_____

_____

_____

• **Superstitious:** 1 Samuel 28:7

_____

_____

_____

_____

• **Ultimately suicidal:** 1 Samuel 31:4

_____

_____

_____

_____

God had fitted Saul for His service, but service takes more than that. A great start—even with God's greatest blessing—does not guarantee a great ending. It requires the person fitting himself for God's service as well. Saul had changed from the humble man to the man from whom the kingdom would be taken. Saul had been chosen by God and anointed by the prophet Samuel, yet he failed to realize that obedience was an absolute necessity.

▶ **16. When we are saved, we become a new creation in Christ; the old is gone, the new has come (see 2 Cor. 5:17 in the margin). With God's help, we must change to be like Christ. After reading the list of Saul's flaws, what are some areas that you know God wants you to change?** _____

_____

_____

2 Corinthians 5:17

"Therefore, if anyone is in Christ, he is a new creation; the old has gone, the new has come!"

What makes this story even more tragic is that God had chosen Saul to be king over Israel. No man could have had a better start as a leader.

 Even though God prepares us to serve Him, we may fail Him by our outright disobedience and/or incomplete obedience. The renewed heart must be anchored close to God.

The importance of a renewed heart also is seen in God replacing Saul with David, a man after His own heart.

PART 4: Saul Replaced by David

▶ **17. Have you been closer to God in the past than you are now? Is it your desire to finish well? What specific things do you need to do to anchor your heart close to God?**

☐ read and study the Bible

☐ serve God through my church

☐ repent of sins

☐ other _____

Saul was told that his kingdom would not last. God had chosen a new leader, one with a special qualification: he was a man after His own heart (1 Sam. 13:14).

After Saul's failure to utterly destroy the Amalakites, Samuel told him again that God had rejected him because of his disobedience. It was a struggle for Saul to accept that he would lose the kingdom. He literally grabbed Samuel's robe and tore it. Samuel then said to him, "The LORD has torn the kingdom of Israel from you today and has given it to one of your neighbors—to one better than you" (1 Sam. 15:28).

Even with all the wrong he had seen in Saul's life, this was a difficult time for Samuel. Finally the Lord said to Samuel, "How long will you mourn for Saul, since I have rejected him as king over Israel? Fill your horn with oil and be on your way; I am sending you to Jesse of Bethlehem. I have chosen one of his sons to be king" (1 Sam. 16:1).

Now the attention turns to David, the man after God's own heart— yet a man whose failures were more enormous than his successes.

► 18. Read Psalm 51:1–12 below.

Have mercy on me, O God,
   according to your unfailing love;
according to your great compassion
   blot out my transgressions.
Wash away all my iniquity
   and cleanse me from my sin.

For I know my transgressions,
   and my sin is always before me.
Against you, you only, have I sinned
   and done what is evil in your sight,
so that you are proved right when you speak
   and justified when you judge.
Surely I was sinful at birth,
   sinful from the time my mother conceived me.
Surely you desire truth in the inner parts;
   you teach me wisdom in the inmost place.

Cleanse me with hyssop, and I will be clean;
   wash me, and I will be whiter than snow.
Let me hear joy and gladness;
   let the bones you have crushed rejoice.
Hide your face from my sins
   and blot out all my iniquity.

Create in me a pure heart, O God,
   and renew a steadfast spirit within me.
Do not cast me from your presence
   or take your Holy Spirit from me.
Restore to me the joy of your salvation
   and grant me a willing spirit, to sustain me.

2 Samuel 24:17

"When David saw the angel who was striking down the people, he said to the LORD, 'I am the one who has sinned and done wrong. These are but sheep. What have they done? Let your hand fall upon me and my family.'"

David's heart was very soft and tender toward God. Though he became terribly self-deceived, even cruel and heartless, he mourned and wept over his sins when God convicted him. David was even willing to give his own life to stay God's hand of judgment on Israel, because he knew that he was responsible for the nation's sinful actions (see 2 Sam. 24:17 in the margin). This is what made him a man after God's heart until the day he died.

God responds to a repentant heart.

When David should have died for his sins of adultery and murder, God responded to his repentant heart. David became a broken man. How reassuring this is when we fail God! The life of David illustrates how much God loves us all. Our Father is gracious and forgiving.

David's life speaks loudly to every person who faces the lure of the world, who is enticed by sin. His successes—but particularly his failures—send warnings we need to heed. The message is loud and clear. It's the same message Paul outlined so succinctly centuries later in his letter to the Galatians:

> *Do not be deceived: God cannot be mocked. A man reaps what he sows. The one who sows to please his sinful nature, from that nature will reap destruction; the one who sows to please the Spirit, from the Spirit will reap eternal life (Gal. 6:7–8).*

In spite of all his failures, David remains one the greatest men of the Bible. He was a man after God's own heart. When God chose David, he chose a man with character, a man whose heart was right toward Him. He was not interested in the size of the man but rather the "size" of his soul.

 To be like David, the first part of your heart examination is to see if you have a renewed heart. Paul makes clear how to have a renewed heart: "If you confess with your mouth, 'Jesus is Lord,' and believe in your heart that God raised him from the dead, you will be saved. For it is with your heart that you believe and are justified, and it is with your mouth that you confess and are saved" (Rom. 10:9–10).

Have you taken this step of faith? If you receive Jesus Christ as your personal Lord and Savior, God will change your heart and give you new life in Christ.

▶ 19. Conclude this chapter with a heart examination.

• Do you have a *renewed* heart? Without a doubt, are you saved?

• Do you have a *receptive* heart? Will you listen to God, His Word, His teachers?

• Do you have a *responsive* heart? As you realize what needs to be changed in your life, do you accept that and make the needed changes?

• What is the *reality* of your heart? Do you reflect a heart for God in your lifestyle? Are you anchored close to God?

Small-Group Meeting 1

Opening Prayer

Begin your time with prayer. Ask God to bless your study together as you seek to understand this lesson from the life of David and apply it to your life.

Building Relationships

This activity helps group members get to know about each other's spiritual lives. Since the emphasis of Lesson 1 is on the renewed heart, ask two or three people to tell about how they became Christians. After the testimonies, ask if anyone can share something specific that changed after he or she was saved.

Reviewing the Lesson

1. Remind the group of the lesson's theme (the renewed heart). Why do you think this study of David begins with looking at the life of Saul? (See the paragraph before #1 on page 10.)

2. What three things were used to prepare Saul to be king? Explain in detail what each was (see Part 2 beginning on page 12).

3. What event prompted Samuel to tell Saul that the kingdom was to be given to another? To see the decline in Saul's life, discuss your answers for #14 on page 16.

4. Discuss #15 on page 17. Read the verses that point out how the various characteristics of Saul were demonstrated in those situations.

Applying the Truths to Life

Select interactive questions to discuss as a group. Some are intended for personal reflection and are not for sharing with the group. Be careful to choose ones that are for open discussion. Include some from each of the four parts of the lesson.

Significant ones to include in this discussion are #1 and #2 (page 10), #7 (page 12), #10 (page 13), and #17 (page 18).

Read aloud the "heart examination" found in #19 on page 20 and allow for a moment or two of meditation.

Ministering to One Another

One of the special blessings of being part of a small group is that you can be aware of each other's needs. Be sure to contact anyone who misses a meeting. Also, be prepared to help members with their needs, whether they need practical help, emotional support, or spiritual instruction.

Reaching Out to Others

You need to decide if your group is an "open" or a "closed" group. Closed groups do not allow others to join after the first few meetings. This allows for group members to develop more openness in what they share.

An open group intends for others to join. If yours is an open group, make sure all understand that. Take time in your first meeting to discuss what you can do specifically to get others to come to your meetings. Every time your group meets, set an extra chair in the room as a reminder of your desire for others to join.

Closing Prayer Time

Distribute sheets of paper to record prayer requests. Encourage everyone to keep these sheets with their study guides and bring them to each group meeting. Encourage them to use these prayer sheets during their private prayer times throughout the week. As members grow more familiar with one another and develop greater trust that confidences will be kept, the requests will become more specific. Remind everyone of the importance of keeping confidences. These prayer times will help the group discover opportunities to minister to one another.

The leader should let the group know who will close the prayer time.

A Dead-End Street Named Self-Confidence

A Reliant Heart

1 Samuel 17

The words "Game Seven" ring with significance to baseball fans. The seventh game of a playoff series is the last shot, do-or-die time for teams in hopes of a championship-clinching victory. Everything is put on the line.

In the 1996 National League Championship Series between the Atlanta Braves and the St. Louis Cardinals, there was a Game Seven. Both teams knew that only one would advance to the World Series. Millions of television viewers watched as into the pressure cooker of the batter's box stepped a 19-year-old. Not a seasoned veteran, nor a perennial all-star, nor a batter with a history of coming through with the clutch hit, but a young man just recently out of high school.

Was the manager crazy? This player had barely proven himself in the minor leagues before he was called up to the majors. The National League pennant was on the line. Advancing to the World Series was at stake. The manager of the Braves was relying on this young player to come through. Atlanta quickly took the lead and essentially won the game in the first inning. How did the 19-year-old do? He became the youngest player to hit a postseason home run. And the Braves became the first team in baseball history to come back from a three-games-to-one deficit to win the NLCS, partly because the manager relied on the ability of young Andruw Jones to do the job.

Upon whom or what do you rely? We may not manage a team into the World Series, but we all experience situations in which the question of whom or what we rely upon is significant.

The temptation is to trust or decide on the basis of what we see or what we can do. We may even have a measure of self-confidence, but, as we'll see in the case of Goliath, that's a dead-end street. What we need is a heart that relies on God.

▶ 1. **What experiences tempt you to trust something or someone other than God? While many situations require that we do something in addition to praying, we must not go to the other extreme and do everything except pray. Here are some needs and the directions** people might look for help. Add to the list and note how reliance on God is important in each situation.

• Health need: trust doctors, try homeopathic remedies, exercise,

_____

• Job need: trust in your resume, network, hire a professional headhunter,

_____

• Family need: see a counselor, attend group therapy session,

_____

• Emotional need: take medication, deny that there is a problem,

_____

• Other _____

▶ 2. In times of need, what are you tempted to trust?

☐ finances   ☐ abilities   ☐ friends

☐ emotions   ☐ Word of God   ☐ prayer

☐ other _____

Often one knows the "right" answer, but what is the "real" answer? In what do you really trust?

_____

   We are learning how to anchor our hearts close to God by looking at the heart of David. In 1 Samuel 17 we see that his heart relied on God. This account teaches us the importance of having—and how to have—a heart that relies on God.

PART 1: Interacting with the Scripture

Reading/Hearing God's Word

▶ 3. Using your Bible, read or listen to the passages of Scripture in the margin. As you begin, ask God to speak to you through His

Read or Listen to:

☐ 1 Samuel 17:32–37

☐ 1 Samuel 17:45–47

Word. Watch for verses or ideas that are especially meaningful to you today. Once you finish reading, check the box indicating the passage(s) you read.

Meditating on God's Word

▶ 4. Write a brief summary of a meaningful verse or idea you just noticed.

_____

_____

_____

1 Samuel 17:45–47

"David said to the Philistine, 'You come against me with sword and spear and javelin, but I come against you in the name of the LORD Almighty, the God of the armies of Israel, whom you have defied. This day the LORD will hand you over to me, and I'll strike you down and cut off your head. Today I will give the carcasses of the Philistine army to the birds of the air and the beasts of the earth, and the whole world will know that there is a God in Israel. All those gathered here will know that it is not by sword or spear that the LORD saves; for the battle is the LORD's, and he will give all of you into our hands.'"

Understanding God's Word

▶ 5. Read again the focal passage for this week's lesson (1 Sam. 17:45–47) in the margin. Underline any key phrases or ideas that seem especially meaningful to you. This will prepare you for the remainder of this week's study.

▶ 6. Look back at this passage. Circle one of the underlined words or phrases that you would like to understand or experience more fully.

Looking through the Scripture to God

Now pause to pray. "Lord, help me see my problems clearly and put them in perspective as David did. I need to understand what really is going on and learn how to rely upon You first and foremost. I need to remember that You expect and enable me to face the challenges of life, but may I do it in Your strength."

PART 2: A Problem of Giant Proportions (1 Sam. 17:1–11)

The Problem Was Real *(vv. 1–4)*

It is too easy to read a passage like this and miss the reality of the situation. For one thing, it was war. The Philistine army had assembled to fight the Israelites. Perhaps modern technology has made warfare seem clinical and distant, but this combat would be mostly hand to hand.

Read these verses again, noticing the geography of the situation. The Philistines were in Judah (see map in the margin). This was an invasion. The enemy was not off in the distance but was camping on Israel's turf!

Add one more thing here. Defeat looked imminent. For more than a month, Goliath had challenged the Israelites to fight. Twice a day, his voice carried across the valley. No one had stepped forward to meet the challenge. The anticipation that hung in the air was of defeat.

The Problem Was Recurring (1 Sam. 13:5; 17:1–7)

God had granted Israel a miraculous victory over the Philistine army. By all human standards, Israel should have been defeated. However, the Lord's blessing was still upon Saul and consequently upon Israel. Even though they were ill equipped for war, God assisted the Israelites by sending an earthquake, creating terrible confusion in the Philistine camp (1 Sam. 14:12–23). Consequently, Israel won an unusual battle.

Routed and defeated, the Philistines reorganized. They desperately wanted to defeat and capture Israel and bring the nation under their dominion. They regrouped and once again "gathered their forces for war" (1 Sam. 17:1). This time, however, they used a different tactic, one that was common in those days. Rather than taking a chance on losing a lot of lives as they did at Micmash, they confronted Israel with a single warrior—Goliath—challenging Saul to send a representative to fight him. The battle would be won or lost on the basis of two men battling each other. The losing side would surrender and voluntarily become servants of the victors.

One of the important lessons to remember is that victories can be followed by renewed battles. When in his spiritual life a believer gains a victory, he must exercise caution. At such a time Satan will strike again. Elijah's triumph over the prophets of Baal was followed by his flight into the wilderness, where he wished to die (1 Kings 19:1–4). The Philistines returned. Sometimes our battles do as well.

► 7. Old habits have amazing staying power. Even after one has resolved to break the habit, the battle can be long and difficult. Sometimes the habit is a sinful pattern that must be changed. What are some non-sinful habits that are difficult for people to stop (e.g., fiddling with coins in pocket while talking to someone)?

_____

_____

_____

What are some sinful habits that are difficult for people to stop (e.g., addictions)?

_____

_____

_____

Finish this sentence: "I know God wants me to stop

_____

The Problem Remained (vv. 8–11)

Twice a day, for 40 days, Goliath descended to the valley floor and shouted up to the children of Israel, challenging someone to come and fight him. His words were clear and crisp—and very foreboding: "Why do you come out and line up for battle? Am I not a Philistine, and are you not the servants of Saul? Choose a man for yourselves and have him come down to me. If he is able to fight and kill me, we will become your subjects; but if I overcome and kill him, you will become our subjects and serve us" (vv. 8–9).

The results were devastating. "On hearing the Philistine's words, Saul and all the Israelites were dismayed and terrified" (v. 11). Not one man in the army of Israel dared to accept the challenge. It would be suicide! Even their leader, Saul—the tallest of them all—was paralyzed with fear.

Sometimes problems remain. The sitcom on television may resolve all problems in less than 30 minutes, but that is not real life. There are times when we say, "I can't go on like this." Still, we need to be people who rely on God. The psalmist reminds us in Psalm 146 that we are to praise the Lord all the time, as long as we live. That includes the tough times as well as the good times.

Our problems may be real, recurring and remain. We need to remember that because even a heart that relies on God will at times have problems of giant proportions.

▶ **8. Read Romans 7:14–25 in the margin. Paul wrote of the struggle with problems that remain. How do long-term problems affect people in the following areas:**

• physical _____

• emotions _____

• spiritual life _____

• relationships _____

Psalm 146:1–2

"Praise the LORD. Praise the LORD, O my soul. I will praise the LORD all my life; I will sing praise to my God as long as I live."

Romans 7:14–25

"We know that the law is spiritual; but I am unspiritual, sold as a slave to sin. I do not understand what I do. For what I want to do I do not do, but what I hate I do. And if I do what I do not want to do, I agree that the law is good. As it is, it is no longer I myself who do it, but it is sin living in me. I know that nothing good lives in me, that is, in my

(continued)

sinful nature. For I have the desire to do what is good, but I cannot carry it out. For what I do is not the good I want to do; no, the evil I do not want to do—this I keep on doing. Now if I do what I do not want to do, it is no longer I who do it, but it is sin living in me that does it.

"So I find this law at work: When I want to do good, evil is right there with me. For in my inner being I delight in God's law; but I see another law at work in the members of my body, waging war against the law of my mind and making me a prisoner of the law of sin at work within my members. What a wretched man I am! Who will rescue me from this body of death?"

2 Corinthians 1:3–4

"Praise be to the God and Father of our Lord Jesus Christ, the Father of compassion and the God of all comfort, who comforts us in all our troubles, so that we can comfort those in any trouble with the comfort we ourselves have received from God."

When you encounter problems of giant proportions, upon whom or what do you rely? In the next part of this chapter, David's reliant heart becomes evident. A heart that relies on God will have a perspective of His provision.

PART 3: David Had a Perspective of God's Provision (1 Sam. 17:12–37)

It Was a Different Perspective (vv. 25–26)

In verse 25 we see the perspective of the "realists." They saw the giant who kept challenging them. They knew the reality of what they faced.

In verse 26, however, we see the perspective of one whom the "realists" considered naïve. David did not see the size of Goliath. He saw the uncircumcised Philistine who was defying the armies of the living God.

David had a different view, and it was not a matter of a realistic view versus a naïve view, either.

▶ 9. How do you view your problems? David's perspective on the Israelites' problem was "different." How can you gain a different perspective that will help with your situation? Read Proverbs 11:14; 12:15; 15:22; 20:18; and 27:17.

_____

_____

_____

▶ 10. What additional perspective can we gain from 2 Corinthians 1:3–4 (in the margin)? In particular, what does God promise to give us during times of trouble? Also, what responsibility comes with God's work in our life at that time?

_____

_____

_____

It Was a Divine Perspective (v. 37a)

The basic question David raises is well stated by Dale Davis in his book *Looking on the Heart:* "Doesn't having a living God make a difference in all this? . . . . Israel thought the Philistine invulnerable; for David he was only uncircumcised. A living God gives a whole new view of things."[1]

Our eyes need to look with a divine perspective on the situations we face. Having a living God does make a difference. As Charles Swindoll notes, "Most people on the battlefield that day saw only one man—Goliath. . . . But David saw the Lord. . . . God was as real to David as Goliath was to the soldiers. But, where the soldiers walked by sight, petrified by Goliath's size, David walked by faith and was moved to obedience by the awesomeness of God's character."[2]

2 Corinthians 5:7

"We live by faith, not by sight."

▶ **11. Read 2 Corinthians 5:7 in the margin. What is the difference between living by faith and living by sight?**

_____

_____

_____

Which is more natural to do?

_____

Which does God want you to do?

_____

David's perspective was not based on just the situation at hand. He remembered how God had delivered him in the past. In particular, he mentioned the times he fought a lion and a bear. Past victories gave him confidence for the present challenge. We, too, need to remember the past victories God has given us as we face our present challenges.

▶ **12. In 1 Samuel 21:8, David asked Ahimelech if there was a spear or sword he could have. The priest answered, "The sword of Goliath." David then said, "There is none like it; give it to me" (v. 9). David wanted the sword because it reminded him of his past victories. What do you have that reminds you of past victories?**

It Was a Determined Perspective (v. 37b)

There were many discouragers in David's life at this point. Eliab, in typical older-brother style, was one. Saul was another. And of course there was Goliath. But all of their words combined did not deter David because he had a determined perspective. His great confidence did not come from his ability, or even from past experiences, but from the knowledge that God would be with him in the battle.

▶ **13. It seems like it is easier to find people who are discouragers rather than encouragers. Which are you?**

_____

A heart that is close to God is a heart that relies on Him.

Write down the name of someone whom you can encourage and what you will do to encourage that person. (This could be a group effort!)

_____

_____

_____

We need to constantly remember the difference that having a living God makes. Too often the words and thoughts of God's people in their times of difficulty sound and look like those of people without God.

▶ 14. *Perseverance, endurance,* and *finishing the course* are all words that indicate determination. Describe how each of the following can help you have a determined perspective.

a. other Christians

_____

b. the Word of God

_____

c. prayer

_____

d. meditation

_____

PART 4: David Proclaimed God's Preeminence (1 Sam. 17:38–54)

God's Preeminence Declared (vv. 38–47)

David both said what he believed and believed what he said. He believed in God's preeminence and declared that by both deed and word.

Saul offered him his armor, but David refused. Without detailing his refusal other than to say that he was not used to the armor, David demonstrated his confidence in God. He would go against the heavily armed Goliath without it. His appearance was one of total vulnerability. David's reliance was not on armor but on God.

▶ 15. **Upon what armor do you rely?**

☐ bank account   ☐ job security   ☐ physical strength

☐ other _____

How do you guard your heart so that your reliance is first of all upon the Lord?

_____

_____

_____

 Declare God's preeminence. Before going further in the study, pray that God would help you show His preeminence in both your words and deeds.

Goliath also got a dose of David's confidence in God. The giant taunted David, insulted the Israelites for sending a boy to fight him, cussed him out, and said that he would feed David to the birds and beasts (vv. 43–44). It was then that David most clearly declared the preeminence of God and showed his reliance on Him. When it was all over, David said, the world would know that there is a God in Israel (v. 46).

God's Preeminence Demonstrated (vv. 48–51)

If actions speak louder than words, what happened next were actions at an earsplitting decibel level. David won a stunning victory. It is an interesting footnote to the biblical account that more verses in this chapter describe the armor of Goliath than the actual battle.

This mighty Philistine warrior had a view of himself and of life that teaches many valuable spiritual lessons:

• Self-Confidence Alone Is a Dead-End Street

Goliath's confidence focused on himself. He placed his faith in his huge frame, his strength, and his ability to wield his weapons.

The Bible describes Goliath's armor in great detail: "He had a bronze helmet on his head and wore a coat of scale armor of bronze weighing five thousand shekels; on his legs he wore bronze greaves, and a bronze javelin was slung on his back. His spear shaft was like a weaver's rod, and its iron point weighed six hundred shekels. His shield bearer went ahead of him" (1 Sam. 17:5–7). A good case seemingly could be made for self-confidence! Goliath had size, strength, and the weapons to go with it.

To the church at Corinth Paul wrote these wise words: "So, if you think you are standing firm, be careful that you don't fall!" (1 Cor. 10:12). Self-confidence can give you a false sense of security. Goliath fell quickly. So can we.

• Arrogance Leads to Disaster

Goliath appeared before Israel with total confidence in his ability to defeat and kill any man who dared to face him on the battlefield. "I defy the ranks of Israel," he shouted (1 Sam. 17:10).

This Philistine warrior was a self-centered man with an ego as big as his body. He believed no man could beat him. He was humiliated when "little David" approached him; it hurt his pride. His arrogance became his downfall! The apostle Paul put it well when he wrote to the Romans, "For by the grace given me I say to every one of you: Do not think of yourself more highly than you ought, but rather think of yourself with sober judgment, in accordance with the measure of faith God has given you" (Rom. 12:3).

• False "Gods" Will Fail Us

When David approached Goliath, the huge Philistine cried out in anger, "'Am I a dog, that you come at me with sticks?' And the Philistine cursed David by *his gods*" (1 Sam. 17:43, emphasis ours). Goliath, like all his compatriots, did not worship the one true God. The Philistines were deeply enmeshed in the Canaanites' religious culture and worshiped false gods such as Dagon and Baal-Zebub (Judges 16:23–24; 1 Sam. 5:1–5; 2 Kings 1:2–6). Sadly, he believed idols made of stone could help him defeat the God who created the universe. He was spiritually blind.

• Tunnel Vision Sets Us Up for Deception

Because of Goliath's human and pagan philosophy of life, he was easily deceived. When David approached him with his shepherd garb and staff and with a mere slingshot in his hand, he threw Goliath off guard. The giant only understood warfare of a certain kind. Like lumbering modern armies facing quick guerrilla fighters, he wasn't prepared to defeat such a simple weapon as a slingshot. He only understood brute strength and how to use "a sword, a spear and a javelin" (1 Sam. 17:45). He suffered from tunnel vision.

Goliath's perspective represents a man of this world. He knew nothing of trusting God and honoring Him with his life. His confidence rested purely in himself, his military skills, and his protective armor. He did not comprehend—or at least refused to acknowledge—the one true God. Consequently, Goliath was extremely vulnerable to a young man who didn't have the warrior's battle skills but who knew how to use a slingshot. More important, David had a dynamic relationship with the living God, upon whom he relied.

How Do We Develop a Reliant Heart?

 People are not born with a reliant heart; it's something we develop. The following steps will help you acquire a heart that relies on God.

a. Remove the confidence that is focused on self alone.

Remember how Goliath's confidence focused on himself? He had a confidence in self alone—his huge frame, his strength, his ability to wield his weapons. In contrast David had both self-confidence and confidence in God. There needs to be a balance of trust and responsibility. David said both that the Lord killed the lion and the bear, and that he had done it. In the battle with Goliath, he knew the battle was the Lord's. On the other hand, he had confidence he could defeat Goliath with his skill with a slingshot.

David knew he had unusual skills. He also knew his limitations. Saul's armor would interfere, not help. He knew he could throw a stone with accuracy. He had honed that skill for years while guarding his father's sheep. He believed his faith in God—combined with his ability to use the sling—would enable him to win the battle against Goliath. And he did!

This is one of the most difficult balances to maintain in life. I (Gene) often find myself vacillating. When I feel good physically and mentally and my ability to produce is high, I tend to place confidence in my own strength. Then I have to experience difficulties and defeat to stop and ask God for His supernatural help.

Some Christians go to two extremes. Either they sit around and wait for God to fight their battles, or they are out trying to win all by themselves. God wants us to balance faith and work in our lives—but always operating in the strength of the Lord! Some people trust in checkbooks and abilities, but we are to trust in the living God.

b. Replace arrogant over-confidence with knowledge of God.

Notice how David remembered what God had done in his life before. When Saul told him that he was not able to fight Goliath, David rehearsed for him what God had done before. "The LORD," he stated, "delivered me from the paw of the lion and the paw of the bear" (1 Sam. 17:37). He knew God in the experiential sense. God had worked in his life in the past, giving him confidence to face what was ahead. "The LORD…will deliver me from the hand of this Philistine." His confidence was not in self alone. Knowing God kept him from relying only on his abilities.

Our opportunities to learn about God are vast. In particular we need to emphasize firsthand knowledge. Read the Bible. Study it. Learn how its lessons apply to real life today. Then live its truths.

Do not try to follow the God of your imagination. Get into the Book and fill your heart and mind with knowledge of God.

c. Remember the victories.

Some saints have very short memories. It has been said that we write our benefits in dust and our injuries in marble. It is equally true that we generally inscribe our afflictions upon brass, while we record the deliverances of God in water. This ought not be. If our memories were more tenacious of the merciful visitations of our God, our faith more often would be strengthened in times of trial.

d. Rely on God.

This is where the proverbial "rubber meets the road." It is the doing of it. Bob Jones Sr., an evangelist from the first part of the 20th century, used to say, "A man is a fool who leans on the arm of flesh when he can be supported by the arm of omnipotence."

David believed in God. While others looked at Goliath and were petrified, David looked by faith at God and was strengthened. Knowing God gave David the courage he needed to rely on Him in the battle with Goliath.

Charles Swindoll challenges us well when he writes: "What about you? Are you a soldier . . . or a David? Do you walk clumsily holding to the flimsy handrail of sight and appearances? Or have you learned to stand firmly on the rock-solid foundation of faith?"[3]

In our achievement-oriented culture, it's easy to carry out tasks in our own strength, not realizing how important it is to trust God to help us. It is easy to bypass God by thinking we can do things in our own strength, calling upon Him only when in over our heads, unable to make it without His help.

God desires that we trust Him at all times. Note His will in this matter as spelled out in the Book of Proverbs: "Trust in the LORD with all your heart and lean not on your own understanding; in all your ways acknowledge him, and he will make your paths straight" (Prov. 3:5–6).

Go back to the story of that baseball player and his manager. What do you think it did to their relationship when the manager relied on the player in that situation? Do you think it created a distance between them, or do you think it might have drawn them closer?

Relying on God always draws us closer to Him.

► **16. The following steps need to be put into practice. Go back over them, thinking through where they apply in your life.**

a. Remove the self-confidence. In what areas of your life does self-confidence demonstrate itself?

_____

_____

_____

b. Replace over-confidence with knowledge of God. Are you learning what the Bible teaches? Do you need to quit some things that are robbing you of the time needed to read and study the Word of God? Take a look at your daily schedule. What needs to change?

_____

_____

_____

c. Remember the victories. Start a "Praise Page." Add it to your prayer list. Regularly write down the victories and praises. What is one praise you could put on that list right now?

_____

_____

_____

d. Rely on God. "Just do it." Is there something right now that you need to commit to God?

_____

_____

_____

Perhaps you can share that in your group and together pray for God's help to rely on Him in that situation.

Small-Group Meeting 2

Opening Prayer

Begin your time together with prayer. Ask God to help you approach this lesson of David and Goliath with an expectant heart that is looking for new lessons from a familiar story.

Building Relationships

Have two or three people tell about an instance when they had to rely on God to help them through a difficult time or make a hard decision. As a follow-up, ask what Scriptures were especially meaningful to each person at that time.

Reviewing the Lesson

1. The theme of this lesson is the reliant heart. Read aloud 1 Samuel 17:1–11, and discuss verse 11. Israel was dismayed and terrified. Could that be the result of relying on themselves instead of God?

2. Israel had a problem of giant proportions. Name the three aspects of that problem and explain each of them (all begin with an "R"—see Part 2 beginning on page 25).

3. To help you understand how real the problem was, look at a map of ancient Israel. How far was it from Jerusalem to the Valley of Elah? Name a city or location that is about the same distance from where you are. What if an invading army were that close to your home?

4. Restate in your own words each aspect of David's perspective (Part 3). More than one group member can help with this question.

What did it mean for him to have:

a. A Different Perspective (1 Sam. 17:25–26)

b. A Divine Perspective (1 Sam. 17:37a)

c. A Determined Perspective (1 Sam. 17:37b)

5. Part 4 of the lesson focuses on God's preeminence. What are the four spiritual lessons learned from Goliath's view of himself and of life?

6. Also from Part 4, what does a person need to do to develop a reliant heart?

Applying the Truths to Life

Select interactive questions from the lesson to discuss as a group. Be careful to choose ones that are for open discussion, since some are intended for personal reflection and are not for sharing with the group. Include some from each of the four parts of the lesson.

Significant ones to include in this discussion are #1 and #2 (pages 23-24), #8, #9, and #10 (pages 27-28), and #12 and #13 (page 29).

Ministering to One Another

Does someone in the group need to rely not only on God but also on you? Read Galatians 6:2 aloud. Perhaps God wants your small group to help bear the burden of another. Ask Him to make you aware of such a need. It might be someone in your group or someone your group knows.

Reaching Out to Others

If yours is an open group, did you set an empty chair in your circle? What will you do to fill it the next time you meet?

Closing Prayer Time

Go through your prayer sheets item by item and ask for updates. The group leader can start keeping a special page of answered prayers. When your group finishes this guide, it will be a special blessing to look over the list of prayer requests that became praises because you prayed! Next, ask for new prayer requests. As the group grows more familiar with one another and develops greater trust that confidences will be kept, the requests will become more specific. Remind everyone of the importance of keeping confidences, and then pray together. These prayer times will help the group discover opportunities to minister to one another.

𝒥rom Faith to Fear and Back
A Reflective Heart

1 Samuel 22:1–2

A little-noticed event took place at the beginning of the 1996 U.S. presidential campaign, one that apparently played a major role in the success of President Clinton's bid to be reelected. It was a repeat of something that worked extremely well in his previous campaign for the presidency: the use of the "War Room."

The "War Room" was the place where a group of strategists and advisors gathered to plan how their candidate would respond to whatever the opposition said.

Their desire was to anticipate the moves of the other candidates. The mechanism was in place to think through and research their response to those moves. It worked—seldom were they caught off guard.

Sometimes in life we can anticipate what is coming and prepare ourselves for it. But other times we are caught by surprise. Our hearts need to be "war room hearts," ones that think through and research our response rather than just react.

The heart anchored close to God will respond rather than react. However, a crucial element is needed for this to happen. The response must come from a reflective heart, one that first turns to God and reflects on who He is and what He desires.

A WWJD ("What Would Jesus Do?") bracelet may remind a person how he is to respond to a situation. But we need more than a bracelet. We need reflective hearts.

> The heart anchored close to God will reflect on who He is and what He desires.

▶ **1. When Israel defeated the Philistines at Mizpah, Samuel took a stone and named it "Ebenezer" to remind them that God had helped them (1 Sam. 7:2–12). Do you have any "Ebenezers"? Name things you have that make you reflect on past blessings.**

_____

_____

_____

David did not always stay strongly on track for God. In his life there was a sequence of wavering, going from certainty to uncertainty, and back to certainty. He moved from faith to fear and back to faith again.

"I find it tremendously comforting," wrote the late Dr. Alan Redpath, "that the Bible never flatters its heroes. It tells the truth about them no matter how unpleasant it may be, so that in considering what is taking place in the shaping of their character we have available all the facts clearly that we may study them."[1]

The obvious unpleasant situation in David's life was his sin of adultery, from which we will learn about his repentant heart. Beginning in 1 Samuel 18, however, is a sequence that occurred earlier than his affair with Bathsheba. It is part of the process of the development of David's character. Initially he moved from faith to fear. But ultimately his life again was one of faith. The vital element in that process was David's reflective heart.

▶ **2. Two things are needed for a person to reflect on God: time and thought. Look over your schedule. How much time daily do you set aside for reading, praying, and thinking about God? Are you spending time with Him individually? Consider also your thoughts. Does your mind tend to wander when you are praying or reading the Bible? Do you practice the discipline of meditation, taking time to focus your thoughts on God and Him alone?**

_____

What are some things in your schedule that you should change to allow more time for God?

_____

_____

What can you do to better focus your thoughts on God?

☐ find a quiet place

☐ eliminate visual distractions

☐ turn off the TV/radio

☐ other _____

_____

_____

Read or Listen to:

☐ 1 Samuel 19:18–24

☐ 1 Samuel 20:1–42

☐ 1 Samuel 21:1–15

☐ Psalm 34

1 Samuel 22:1–2

"David left Gath and escaped to the cave of Adullam. When his brothers and his father's household heard about it, they went down to him there. All those who were in distress or in debt or discontented gathered around him, and he became their leader. About four hundred men were with him."

PART 1: Interacting with the Scripture

Reading/Hearing God's Word

▶ 3. Using your Bible, read or listen to the passages of Scripture in the margin. As you begin, ask God to speak to you through His Word. Watch for verses or ideas that are especially meaningful to you today. Once you finish reading, check the box indicating the passage(s) you read.

_____

_____

_____

Meditating on God's Word

▶ 4. Write a brief summary of a meaningful verse or idea you noticed.

_____

_____

_____

Understanding God's Word

▶ 5. Read again the focal passage for this week's lesson (1 Sam. 22:1–2) in the margin along with Psalm 34. Underline any key phrases or words that seem especially meaningful to you. This will prepare you for the remainder of this week's study.

▶ 6. Look back at this passage. Circle a key word or phrase that you would like to understand or experience more fully.

Looking through the Scripture to God

Now pause to pray. "God, help me to quiet my heart as I study this lesson. Pressures and difficulties in life can drive me to fear. Help me steady my heart and learn to live by faith. May David's example teach me how to accomplish this in my life."

PART 2: Living by Reacting Can Put Us on the Running Track

The Spirit of the Lord was upon David in a mighty way. Against impossible odds, he faced Goliath and killed him, which was only the beginning of his great exploits in doing battle against the Philistines. He was known in Israel as a man of unusual courage and great faith in God.

But all was not well in David's heart and life. A change was gradually taking place. Little by little his faith in God's protection was being replaced by fear of what one man could do to him. And that man was King Saul.

▶ 7. Whom or what do you fear? Faith can ebb and flow, usually in direct proportion to the challenge you are facing, whether real or imagined. What is in your life right now that is moving you from faith to fear?

_____

_____

_____

David's fear was understandable, even predictable. He had faithfully served Saul as one of his armor-bearers and as his personal musician. At one time the king had demonstrated great love toward him (1 Sam. 16:21). But when David was honored by the people of Israel for his great victory over Goliath, Saul's love turned to intense jealousy, anger, and suspicion. He actually looked for opportunities to kill David (1 Sam. 18:9–29).

Foiled in his murder attempts, Saul planned David's death on the battlefield by giving him greater military responsibility. Again, Saul's scheme failed. Repeatedly, he tried to "pin David to the wall" with his spear, but each time David escaped. Saul's anger became relentless. He sent his men to kill David. But David, with his wife's help, escaped through a window and fled (1 Sam. 19:1–12).

Saul's attempts on David's life were becoming more frequent and intense. It was no longer a private scheme but a public strategy. And no one, including God, would blame David for fleeing from Saul's presence. It was the only sensible thing to do.

There is no doubt David was under tremendous pressure. Few men would have—or could have—handled the situation the way he did. God certainly understood these difficulties.

▶ 8. Sometimes other people put us under pressure to get us to do what they want. How do you respond?

☐ cave in to the pressure   ☐ lash out at the person

☐ passively resist   ☐ get away/avoid the person

☐ determine to do what God wants

☐ other _____

When David took matters into his own hands, things went from bad to worse.

However, there is another perspective. How David responded inwardly to these pressures and, more significantly, how he responded to God's protection is another matter. Rather than trusting the Lord as he had done so frequently in difficult situations, he began to lose his spiritual and emotional bearings. His most serious mistake occurred when he ignored God's protection and took matters into his own hands. When he did, things went from bad to worse.

▶ 9. **Look at the following situations and note how the people took things into their own hands.**

a. Moses (Num. 20:1–12) _____

_____

b. the people of Israel (Num. 14:44–45) _____

_____

What were the results of their actions?

a. Moses _____

_____

b. the people of Israel _____

_____

David's First Scheme

David first attempted to solve his problem by issuing an order to Jonathan, Saul's son and his best friend: "Look, tomorrow is the New Moon festival, and I am supposed to dine with the king; but let me go and hide in the field until the evening of the day after tomorrow. If your father misses me at all, tell him, 'David earnestly asked my permission to hurry to Bethlehem, his hometown, because an annual sacrifice is being made there for his whole clan.' If he says, 'Very well,' then your servant is safe. But if he loses his temper, you can be sure that he is determined to harm me" (1 Sam. 20:5–7).

At least three things were wrong with this scheme. First, where was God in this plan? In devising this scheme, David didn't consult the Lord at all. In fact, His name isn't even mentioned in the plan.

How opposite from David's attitude and actions when he faced Goliath! At that time he said to Saul with great confidence, "The LORD who delivered me from the paw of the lion and the paw of the bear will deliver me from the hand of this Philistine" (1 Sam. 17:37). And when he encountered the giant face to face, David shouted, "I come against you *in the name of the LORD Almighty,* the *God* of the armies of Israel. . . . This day the LORD will hand you over to me . . . and the whole world will know that there is a *God* in Israel. All those gathered here will know that it is not by sword or spear that the LORD saves; for the battle is the LORD'S, and *he* will give all of you into our hands" (vv. 45–47, emphasis ours).

▶ **10. Whom or what do you consult in a pressure situation? Check all the ones that apply and compare them with David's course of action.**

☐ friends   ☐ astrology charts   ☐ pastor

☐ talk show host   ☐ self

☐ other _____

Second, what happened to David's God-consciousness? Somehow, David lost his spiritual bearings. The David we once knew would have said to Jonathan that day, "This struggle between your father and me is the Lord's. He will deliver me just as He did in Ramah." Instead, he came up with his own scheme. He left God out of the picture.

▶ **11. How do you keep God in mind?**

☐ pray regularly during the day

☐ with an "Ebenezer," a visible reminder of God's importance in my life

☐ acknowledge dependence on God when talking to others

☐ other _____

☐ I don't

Third, there was an element of dishonesty in David's strategy. True, he may have planned to go to Bethlehem to sacrifice with his family someday, but there's no evidence he ever did or that he really planned to go at that moment. Furthermore, David asked Jonathan to give the impression he had already gone to Bethlehem (1 Sam. 20:27–29), when in reality he was waiting in the field for a report on Saul's behavior (v. 24).

This was just the beginning of David's verbal distortions. One lie often leads to another—and this is exactly what happened to David. In Ephesians 4:25, Paul gives us an important principle regarding what we say. We are to "put off falsehood and speak truthfully."

Ephesians 4:25

"Therefore each of you must put off falsehood and speak truthfully to his neighbor, for we are all members of one body."

▶ **12. What are your words worth? Can you be "taken at your word"? Commit to being a person of your word. What are some specific areas in which you need to reconsider your words?**

☐ excuses for missed work

☐ income tax forms

☐ why a project was turned in late

☐ explanation given to a spouse, a parent, a coworker

☐ other _____

David's Second Scheme

Though David's scheme was purely a human strategy, it achieved its purpose. Saul's anger raged so out of control when he discovered David wasn't coming to his special luncheon that he attempted to kill Jonathan instead (1 Sam. 20:33). But his son escaped and went into the field to deliver the bad news to his friend. In David's mind, he had no choice. Once again he fled—this time to the tabernacle in Nob.

▶ **13. Saul's frustrations resulted in angry actions. How do you deal with your frustrations?**

☐ take them out on others

☐ address what is causing the frustration and solve the problem

☐ push through to get what I want

☐ pray and think before speaking and acting

☐ do a "slow burn"

Ahimelech, the priest, was surprised to see David—especially since he was traveling alone (1 Sam. 21:1). In his panic, David once again took matters into his own hands. He took advantage of Ahimelech's surprise and quickly fabricated another story: "The king charged me with a certain matter and said to me, 'No one is to know anything about your mission and your instructions.' As for my men, I have told them to meet me at a certain place" (v. 2). In other words, he gave Ahimelech the false impression that he was alone because he was on a secret mission for King Saul.

This time, however, things didn't work out as nicely as David had hoped. Though he fooled Ahimelech, one of Saul's chief shepherds, Doeg the Edomite, also was in Nob that day and saw David. Word soon got back to Saul about David's conversation with the priest in Nob (1 Sam. 22:9–10).

The results of David's sin in this case were tragic. Saul immediately called for Ahimelech and his whole family of priests. The king was irate and irrational. He accused Ahimelech of protecting David and helping him escape. No explanation would suffice. He ordered Ahimelech's death as well as the death of all the priests present that day—85 men (v. 18). The king also ordered an attack on Nob, and his men killed "the town of the priests, with its men and women, its children and infants, and its cattle, donkeys and sheep" (v. 19). They wiped out the entire city!

All this happened because David took matters into his own hands and lied. Later he acknowledged to a lone survivor, Abiathar, that he was responsible for the death of everyone in "your father's whole family" (v. 23). He took responsibility, but the damage was done. One sin led to another, then to tragedy. David escaped because of his scheme, but in the process he caused the death of hundreds of innocent people. What a price to pay for disobedience and lack of trust in God!

1 Corinthians 10:31–32

"So whether you eat or drink or whatever you do, do it all for the glory of God. Do not cause anyone to stumble, whether Jews, Greeks or the church of God."

1 Peter 2:12

"Live such good lives among the pagans that, though they accuse you of doing wrong, they may see your good deeds and glorify God on the day he visits us."

▶ **14. David's second scheme cost many innocent people their lives. The results of our sins may not be as drastic, but we must realize that our sins affect others (see 1 Cor. 10:31–32 and 1 Pet. 2:12 in the margin). Indicate how these sins affect others:**

a. lying _____

_____

b. alcoholism _____

_____

c. shoplifting _____

_____

d. sexual immorality _____

_____

David's Third Scheme

Before David learned from his mistakes—before he even learned about the death of the people in Nob—he concocted yet another scheme. This time his behavior was even more bizarre.

David left Nob and headed into enemy territory, hoping he no longer would be recognized as a warrior in Israel. But he was wrong. The servants of Achish, king of Gath, noticed him (1 Sam. 21:10–11).

David's anxiety now reached almost unbearable proportions. We're told he was "very much afraid of Achish" (v. 12). David panicked and feigned madness. In a pathetic portrayal of insanity, he made "marks on the doors of the gate and [let] saliva run down his beard" (v. 13). Could this be the one God had called "a man after his own heart"?

Again, David's scheme worked—at least he escaped injury.

▶ **15. One sin can easily lead to another, ensnaring your life in a downward spiral. Go back over the list of sins in Activity 14 and indicate below how each might start with a small action and yet become significant.**

a. lying _____

_____

b. alcoholism _____

_____

c. shoplifting _____

_____

d. sexual immorality _____

_____

Finally, David found himself in a lonely cave, where he began to reflect on his bizarre and sinful behavior. There in the darkness, he once again began to focus his heart and mind on the Lord (1 Sam. 22:1–2).

PART 3: Living by Reflecting Can Put Us on the Right Track

When David stopped running and scheming, he reflected on his situation and his Lord. No longer reacting, he responded to his circumstances by turning to God.

In the language of today, it might be said that David spent his time journaling. He recorded his thoughts. Realize, though, that what he wrote was inspired by the Holy Spirit. The psalms written during that period in the cave are indicated as such by their titles. For example, in Psalm 142 he cried out to God, and in Psalm 57:2 he remembered God's purpose for him.

▶ **16. Two spiritual disciplines that can help develop and maintain a reflective heart are meditation and journaling. During the next week, set aside several periods of time to read and meditate on one of the psalms mentioned in this lesson. As each of those periods** concludes, write out a prayer of response to the psalm along with the things God is impressing on your heart.

David's new perspective was evident in Psalms 27 and 31.

"Whom Shall I Fear?"
Psalm 27:1-3
The LORD is my light and my salvation—
    whom shall I fear?
The LORD is the stronghold of my life—
    of whom shall I be afraid?
When evil men advance against me
    to devour my flesh,
when my enemies and my foes attack me,
    they will stumble and fall.
Though an army besiege me,
    my heart will not fear;
though war break out against me,
    even then will I be confident.

▶ **17. Ask yourself these two very important questions:**

a. Do I know God? (Do I have a renewed heart?)   ☐ yes ☐ no

b. Do I truly rely on God? (Do I have a reliant heart?)   ☐ yes ☐ no

"You Are My Rock . . . My Fortress . . . My Strength"
Psalm 31:1–5
In you, O LORD, I have taken refuge;
    let me never be put to shame;
    deliver me in your righteousness.
Turn your ear to me,
    come quickly to my rescue;
Be my rock of refuge,
    a strong fortress to save me.
Since you are my rock and my fortress,
    for the sake of your name lead and guide me.
Free me from the trap that is set for me,
    for you are my refuge.
Into your hands I commit my spirit;
    redeem me, O LORD, the God of truth.

Psalm 31 is a prayer of trust and commitment. At the conclusion of this study time, sit quietly, reflect on the words of this psalm, read them aloud, and then pray. Ask God to help you commit your spirit into His hand.

The dark cave of Adullam was a much different environment from the hillsides of Judea, where David cared for his father's sheep and enjoyed an intimate relationship with his Maker. But it provided an aura in which to grasp the darkness that had captured his soul. Once again the light of God's revelation brightened his outlook on life and brought him a sense of inner security. The sunlight of God's love and care diffused his profound fear and refocused his bizarre thoughts. David once again trusted God rather than relying on his skills and abilities. And once again he faced his problems with a divine perspective.

Events will sometimes bring us to our own cave of Adullam. In those times we need to listen and learn from God. Our actions must come from hearts that reflect on Him.

► **18. When you need a quiet place in which to reflect, where do you go? Your favorite place for a personal retreat does not need to be one for extended stay or be a long ways from home. A chair by the fireplace or a bench in the backyard can work. If you do not have a retreat place, pick one now and decide when you will go there to reflect on this lesson.**

_____

_____

_____

PART 4: What Had David Learned?

We're not told how long it took David to confess his sins and experience a restored fellowship with God. However, we know it eventually happened. Psalm 34 speaks volumes, since David probably composed these thoughts while sitting alone in that cave. Read this psalm against the backdrop of what we've learned about David's sins; it is self-explanatory.

Remain Humble!

I will extol the LORD at all times;

    his praise will always be on my lips.

My soul will boast in the LORD;

    let the afflicted hear and rejoice.

Glorify the LORD with me,

    let us exalt his name together.

Keep Praying!

I sought the LORD, and he answered me;
    he delivered me from all my fears.
Those who look to him are radiant;
    their faces are never covered with shame.
This poor man called, and the LORD heard him;
    he saved him out of all his troubles.
The angel of the LORD encamps around those who fear Him,
    and he delivers them.

Trust God!

Taste and see that the LORD is good;
    blessed is the man who takes refuge in him.
Fear the LORD, you his saints;
    for those who fear him lack nothing.
The lions may grow weak and hungry;
    but those who seek the LORD lack no good thing.

Be Honest!

Come, my children, listen to me;
    I will teach you the fear of the LORD.
Whoever of you loves life,
    and desires to see many good days,
keep your tongue from evil
    and your lips from speaking lies.
Turn from evil and do good;
    seek peace and pursue it.

Be Righteous!

The eyes of the LORD are on the righteous
    and his ears are attentive to their cry;
the face of the LORD is against those who do evil,
    to cut off the memory of them from the earth.
The righteous cry out, and the LORD hears them;
    he delivers them from all their troubles.
The LORD is close to the brokenhearted
    and saves those who are crushed in spirit.

Rest in God!

A righteous man may have many troubles,
  but the LORD delivers him from them all;
he protects all his bones,
  not one of them will be broken.
Evil will slay the wicked;
  the foes of the righteous will be condemned.
The LORD redeems his servants;
  no one will be condemned who takes refuge in him.

► **19. Trying to walk with God on the run will not get you where you need to be spiritually. The hectic life will not be the reflective life. Consider these opportunities for reflection:**

• The quiet of morning. Get up a little earlier.

• The quiet of the commute. Turn off the radio.

• The quiet of the break. Find an isolated place at work.

• The quiet of the evening. Turn off the TV.

• The quiet of a path. Take a walk or run and commune with God.

You need a place you can go to with a purpose and a plan in mind. Remember, it was a time of reflection that pulled David out of his downward spiritual spiral.

Small-Group Meeting 3

Opening Prayer

Begin this meeting with a time of silent prayer. Allow everyone to go "one on one" with God for a moment, asking Him to help them develop a reflective heart. The leader, or someone appointed by the leader, can bring this time of silent prayer to a conclusion by praying aloud.

Building Relationships

We all have stress in our lives. Often in times of stress the "real you" makes an appearance! Ask if someone has a story to share about a time that a stressful situation brought about a wrong response. Caution the group to think carefully about what they relate, since no one should be embarrassed by the story that is told. Also, you could ask some to relate a story about how God specifically led them through a stressful situation.

Reviewing the Lesson

1. The theme of this lesson is the reflective heart. As a way of beginning to challenge the group about the importance of having such a heart, discuss the fact that the busyness of our lives can keep us from having a reflective heart. What can we do to make time to just sit and think?

2. Read aloud 1 Samuel 19:1. What were some of the ways Saul tried to kill David or have him killed?

3. In Part 2 the three schemes of David are described. Ask different members to tell what each scheme was and what was wrong with it.

4. Read aloud 1 Samuel 22:1. Why was the cave of Adullam a good place for reflecting?

5. In Part 4 you will find the words of Psalm 34 with specific lessons. Take turns reading a section of the psalm and pointing out how that portion of the psalm relates to the specific lesson mentioned.

Applying the Truths to Life

Select interactive questions from this lesson to discuss as a group. Be careful to choose ones that are for open discussion, since some are intended for personal reflection and are not for sharing with the group. Include some from each of the four parts of the lesson.

Specifically talk about #17 on page 46. Encourage everyone to keep a journal for the next few weeks. Talk about what you might write in one, such as special thoughts from your devotions, insights from God's Word into events of that day, blessings, and special prayer requests.

Activity #19 (page 49) is good for discussing when to have a quiet time. It may be that some in the group do not regularly spend time reading the Bible and praying. Be sensitive to that possibility and use the opportunity to encourage daily devotions.

Ministering to One Another

Ask group members to relate some of the opportunities they've had to help bear the burden of someone else. (Their examples do not have to be about how they helped someone who is part of your group.) Next, talk about some specific thing that members could do for others in the coming week.

Reaching Out to Others

If yours is an open group, did you set an empty chair in your circle? What will you do to fill it the next time you meet? Remember, if you do not plan for it, your group probably won't grow. In the closing prayer time, pray for people by name whom you will invite to the next group meeting.

Closing Prayer Time

Review your prayer sheets and ask for updates. Then allow members to share new prayer requests. Encourage members to be open with the group, but remind everyone of the importance of keeping confidences.

Keeping from Caving In
A Restrained Heart

1 Samuel 24:1–22; 26:1–25

Edgar Allan Poe wrote a classic story on revenge entitled "The Cask of Amontillado." The story opens with the words, "The thousand injuries of Fortunato I had borne as I best could, but when he ventured upon insult I vowed revenge."

What follows is a brief treatise on vengeance. Poe wrote of an intent to "not only punish but punish with impunity." Along with that were two other key elements. The best revenge, according to Poe, is when the person knows that it is happening to him and he cannot do anything about it or do anything to retaliate. The story then details just such a scenario.

Too often people tend to favor revenge over restraint. We like the long-standing rivalries, the athletic contests with "bad blood" between the teams. *Payback* is not only a movie title, but viewing it was a vicarious experience for some. The language of American folklore includes the Hatfields and the McCoys. The bumper sticker philosophy in our society is, "I don't get mad, I get even."

▶ **1. Is there anyone with whom you want to get even? Ask God to help you think this through carefully before continuing on in the study. Pray that He would keep that person's face in your mind as you read about David's restraint.**

Some people have hearts that carry resentment, while others take it a step further, looking for opportunities to get their revenge. What seems to be lacking are hearts that have a proper sense of restraint, especially when faced with resentful people or surrounded by revengeful people. Resentment and revenge can pull a heart away from God. But the heart anchored close to God will be one of restraint.

David was in this exact situation. The restraint of his heart kept him from drifting away and being swept along by the twin tides of resentment and revenge.

PART 1: Interacting with the Scripture

Reading/Hearing God's Word

▶ 2. Using your Bible, read or listen to the passages of Scripture listed in the margin. As you begin, ask God to speak to you through His Word. Watch for verses or ideas that are especially meaningful to you today. Once you finish reading, check the box indicating the passage(s) you read.

Read or Listen to:

☐ 1 Samuel 24:1–22

☐ 1 Samuel 26:1–25

☐ Matthew 5:43–48

☐ Romans 12:18–19

Meditating on God's Word

▶ 3. Write a brief summary of a meaningful verse or idea you noticed.

_____

_____

_____

Understanding God's Word

▶ 4. Read again the focal passage for this week's lesson (1 Sam. 24:5–12) in the margin. Underline any key phrases or words that seem especially meaningful to you.

▶ 5. Look back at this passage. Circle a key word or phrase that you would like to understand or experience more fully.

Looking through the Scripture to God

 Now pause to pray. "Father, I know there are times when I want to get back at someone else. It may be something as silly as getting even when cut off in traffic. Still, my response is one of desiring revenge. Help me learn from David to leave all my offenses in Your hands. Give me a heart of restraint."

PART 2: Saul Had a Heart of Resentment (1 Sam. 24:1–2)

After his battle with the Philistines, Saul once again discovered David's location. And once again the king pursued David, this time taking 3,000 of his best warriors with him. Saul's behavior demonstrates vividly how bitterness can twist a man's soul. His heart was hard and his ears were deaf to God's sovereign will. Hardly home from battle, he went out after David again.

1 Samuel 24:5–12

"Afterward, David was conscience-stricken for having cut off a corner of his robe. He said to his men, 'The LORD forbid that I should do such a thing to my master, the LORD's anointed, or lift my hand against him; for he is the anointed of the LORD.' With these words David rebuked his men and did not allow them to attack Saul. And Saul left the cave and went his way.

"Then David went out of the cave and called out to Saul, 'My lord the king!' When Saul looked behind him, David bowed down and prostrated himself with his face to the ground. He said to Saul, 'Why do you listen when men say, "David is bent on harming you"? This day you have seen with your own eyes how the LORD delivered you into my

(continued)

hands in the cave. Some urged me to kill you, but I spared you; I said, "I will not lift my hand against my master, because he is the LORD's anointed." See, my father, look at this piece of your robe in my hand! I cut off the corner of your robe but did not kill you. Now understand and recognize that I am not guilty of wrongdoing or rebellion. I have not wronged you, but you are hunting me down to take my life. May the LORD judge between you and me. And may the LORD avenge the wrongs you have done to me, but my hand will not touch you.'"

► 6. Do you remember this old adage: "Idle hands are the devil's workshop"? When Saul had free time, he turned back to pursuing David. Keeping busy with worthwhile activities will not automatically keep us out of trouble, but it helps. Name some ways to use your free time that will help you grow spiritually.

_____

_____

_____

The Reasons for His Resentment

There were two basic reasons for Saul's resentment of David. The first was that David was his successor. In a monarchy, successors are born into the line of succession, not brought in by anointing. Saul's failure to obey (1 Sam. 13:8–14) resulted in God removing the throne from him. His son Jonathan was next in line until God's judgment fell. Consequently, he resented David.

The second reason was that David was successful. Saul knew success. The people sang of how he had slain his thousands. Israel was experiencing military victories and Saul was their leader.

But the people had a second verse in their song: David had slain his ten thousands (1 Sam. 21:11). Instead of celebrating the success of David, the song was a cause for resentment. Not only was Saul losing the position of power but also the praise of the people. God was blessing David, not him.

► 7. Envy and jealousy are twin monsters that grow to gargantuan proportions when fed a steady diet of comparison and self-pity. Both are mentioned in Galatians 5:19–21 as "acts of the sinful nature." What should you do to keep that from happening in your life?

_____

_____

_____

A Relentless Resentment

Saul's resentment ultimately manifested itself in actions. The king wanted David dead. He relentlessly pursued that goal by attempting to kill David personally (1 Sam. 18:10–11; 19:10), by attempting to have David killed by the Philistines (18:25), and by attempting to kill David by pursuing him as seen in this passage. It was as if he said in his heart, "One way or another, David will die."

Saul's behavior is a striking example of how envy and jealousy can so adversely affect a person's attitude toward others. It's as if the person becomes deaf and no longer hears the Word of God. The hard heart refuses to relent.

No one is immune from the possibility of this happening in his own heart. As Kenneth Chafin observes in his commentary on this passage, "When I study the Scriptures I try to find myself in the stories. Even as I have written about Saul's hatred of David, I have thought of people who hate me and who try to do me harm. And as I have written about David's transparency in his efforts to be reconciled to Saul, I think of those times I have reached out to people without success. But even as I had these thoughts I had to admit that I wasn't being entirely honest with myself. For just as often I have played Saul's role."[1]

Is this your heart?

 Now pause to pray. "Search me, O God, and know my heart; test me and know my anxious thoughts. See if there is any offensive way in me, and lead me in the way everlasting" (Ps. 139:23–24). Then sit silently for a moment, waiting for God to answer. If you already think you know what "way" He will point out, then the prayer is already answered. What should you do with the answers to this prayer?

_____

_____

PART 3: David's Men Had a Heart of Revenge (1 Sam. 24:3–4a)

What happened next is ironic but revealing. David and his little band took refuge in the desert of En Gedi, a place designated as the "Crags of the Wild Goats" (1 Sam. 24:2). Dozens of caverns and caves were in this area; one was so large that it once sheltered 30,000 people from a terrible storm.[2] Many believe this was the cave David used as a hiding place from Saul.

If it weren't so pathetic, this scene would be almost humorous. While searching for David, Saul took refuge from the hot sun in the same cave where David and his men were hiding. Lurking in the shadows, they were invisible to Saul. The king thought he was alone.

David's men were overjoyed; here was his golden opportunity. In fact, they actually interpreted what was happening as the Lord's provision. Thus they said to David, "This is the day the LORD spoke of when he said to you, 'I will give your enemy into your hands for you to deal with as you wish'" (v. 4).

Apparently, David's men were paraphrasing some of his psalms. Perhaps they were referring to their previous experience in the cave of Adullam, when David had written, "The face of the LORD is against those who do evil, to cut off the memory of them from the earth" (Ps. 34:16). It's not surprising that they saw in this "cave experience" a grand opportunity to help the Lord eliminate David's greatest foe.

▶ **8. David's men encouraged him to cave in to the temptation to harm Saul. Indicate how our enemy can use each of the following to encourage us to get revenge.**

a. Society's emphasis on getting even.

_____

_____

b. Friends who take up our offenses.

_____

_____

c. Examples in entertainment where the featured character gets revenge.

_____

_____

It looked providential to David's men. As they saw it, the situation in which they found themselves had all the markings of God's handiwork. There was no question in their mind regarding the will of God. With their words, masked by a veil of spirituality, they encouraged David to retaliate.

There is no indication that David was looking for an opportunity to get back at Saul. At the same time there is nothing to show what David was doing to keep from developing that desire. Revenge may develop quietly in one's heart. As Charles Swindoll puts it, "Revenge surreptitiously wraps its thistly branches around all of us. And when it does, even the most forgiving, most peaceful of people will become beasts."[3]

James 3:3–12

"When we put bits in the mouths of horses to make them obey us, we can turn the whole animal. Or take ships as an example. Although they are so large and are driven by strong winds, they are steered by a very small rudder wherever the pilot wants to go. Likewise the tongue is a small part of the body, but it makes great boasts. Consider what a great forest is set on fire by a small spark. The tongue also is a fire, a world of evil among the parts of the body. It corrupts the whole person, sets the whole course of his life on fire, and is itself set on fire by hell.

"All kinds of animals, birds, reptiles and creatures of the sea are being tamed and have been tamed by man, but no man can tame the tongue. It is a restless evil, full of deadly poison.

"With the tongue we praise our Lord and Father, and with it we curse men, who have been made in God's likeness. Out of the same mouth come praise and cursing. My brothers, this should not be. Can both fresh water and salt water flow from the same spring? My brothers, can a fig tree bear olives, or a grapevine bear figs? Neither can a salt spring produce fresh water."

▶ 9. Read James 3:3–12 in the margin aloud.

To what three things does James compare the tongue?

_____

_____

_____

How can the tongue be used for revenge?

_____

_____

_____

▶ 10. Sometimes people reason, "As long as I only think it, it is all right." Read Matthew 5:21–22 below.

"'You have heard that it was said to the people long ago, "Do not murder, and anyone who murders will be subject to judgment." But I tell you that anyone who is angry with his brother will be subject to judgment. Again, anyone who says to his brother, "Raca," is answerable to the Sanhedrin. But anyone who says, "You fool!" will be in danger of the fire of hell."'

What would Jesus say to them?

_____

_____

_____

Is this your heart?

Before moving on to the next section, take time to pray the prayer of David that is found at the end of Psalm 139 (in the margin on the next page). Ask God if there is "any offensive way" in you, any heart of resentment. Spend a few moments in quiet and carefully note what comes to mind. It may be that God's Word and your prayer will help you realize those whom you resent.

_____

_____

_____

PART 4: David Had a Heart of Restraint (1 Sam. 24:4b–22)

Other people encouraged David to vindicate himself by taking Saul's life. How easy it would have been for him to take their advice! Some of his most trusted men believed revenge was the right thing to do. But David demonstrated true character when he stood strong against the tide of opinion. He knew harming Saul would be wrong—period. He held fast to his convictions.

▶ **11. Upon what resources do you draw when tempted to cave in?**

☐ Scripture

☐ support of a friend

☐ fear of what might happen

☐ other _____

He Refused to Give In

David demonstrated true character when he stood strong against the tide of opinion to harm Saul, even though there was no question that he had a right to defend himself against the king.

As David watched Saul sleeping, he must have remembered the times the king tried to pin him to the wall with his spear. He must have thought of the times Saul sent him into battle against the Philistines, hoping he would be killed. And how could he forget the times Saul nearly captured him with his well-trained army?

What an opportunity to avenge himself! The temptation was great—and David seemingly took some initial steps to carry out what appeared to be an opportunity from the Lord to put an end to this struggle.

▶ **12. Is opportunity always a clear indication of God's will? Support your answer from 1 Samuel 24.**

_____

_____

_____

To draw this conclusion, however, we have to read between the lines. Apparently Saul fell asleep in the coolness of the cave. While he dozed, David crept up on Saul and "cut off the edge" of his robe (1 Sam. 24:4).

The Hebrew word *kanap,* used in verse 4, means "wing" or "extremity." David probably cut off just a corner of the hem of Saul's robe. This was a symbol of disloyalty and rebellion, whereas "to seize the hem of a garment" was a symbol of faith, loyalty, and covenant making.[4]

David's refusal to give in to revenge was twofold. First, he refused to kill his adversary because Saul was much more than that. In his own words David acknowledged that Saul was anointed of the Lord (v. 6). Once anointed, the individual was set apart or consecrated to God.

▶ **13. Is respect for God's leaders important today? Read Hebrews 13:17 and 1 Timothy 5:17–20 in the margin and note how they apply to your relationship with your pastor and other spiritual leaders.**

_____

_____

_____

Second, David refused to seize the kingdom. He honored Saul even though the king was out of the will of God. The man after God's own heart did not seize the kingship promised but waited for it to be given to him.

Jesus faced the same test. Satan said to Him, "All this [the kingdoms of the world] I will give you if you will bow down and worship me" (Matt. 4:9). But Jesus refused because He knew that God's will must come to pass in God's way.

Think for a moment about what happened. How easily David could have interpreted these opportunities to take Saul's life as chances provided by the Lord Himself. How easy this act of revenge would have been to rationalize, particularly since David knew it was God's plan for him to replace Saul as king. From a human point of view, David could have positioned himself as victor and every soldier in Israel would have rallied to support him—especially since they were well aware of Saul's unpredictable personality and inconsistent behavior.

David, however, did not yield to those tempting thoughts. He knew it wouldn't be right for him to take matters into his own hands and harm Saul.

Hebrews 13:17

"Obey your leaders and submit to their authority. They keep watch over you as men who must give an account. Obey them so that their work will be a joy, not a burden, for that would be of no advantage to you."

1 Timothy 5:17–20

"The elders who direct the affairs of the church well are worthy of double honor, especially those whose work is preaching and teaching. For the Scripture says, 'Do not muzzle the ox while it is treading out the grain,' and 'The worker deserves his wages.' Do not entertain an accusation against an elder unless it is brought by two or three witnesses. Those who sin are to be rebuked publicly, so that the others may take warning."

He Acted Righteously

In a situation that could bring out the lesser in a man, David demonstrated the greater qualities. In essence, he acted righteously.

His actions were restrained. It was within David's grasp to physically harm, even kill Saul. But he did neither.

His attitude was humble, even though he easily could have ridiculed Saul. While his actions were restrained, his address to the king was respectful (1 Sam. 24:8). David bowed down, even prostrated himself before Saul. His statement of what had just transpired (vv. 9–15) is additional evidence of David's righteous actions and attitude.

▶ **14. How do you respond to those who attack you?**

☐ retaliate with an attack on them

☐ burn quietly on the inside

☐ bide my time for a good opportunity to get back at them

☐ commit the situation to Christ in prayer

☐ sabotage their projects

☐ act piously

☐ other _____

When Saul awakened and left the cave, David followed and called after him. With sincere humility and deep respect, he pleaded with Saul, "Why do you listen when men say, 'David is bent on harming you'?" (v. 9). To demonstrate his own pure motives, he held up the piece of Saul's robe, proving he had no intention of killing him.

Even Saul acknowledged David's righteousness. The king knew instantly what had happened. David had an opportunity to kill him but spared his life. There was no way he could misconstrue the facts. Looking at his robe and the missing piece, he knew David could have severed his head with one stroke. He was humbled. He wept before David and confessed his wickedness. He acknowledged that God had delivered him into David's hands and yet David had not killed him.

For a moment, we see a man moved to tears. Saul was overwhelmed with David's mercy. "When a man finds his enemy, does he let him get away unharmed?" the king asked. "May the LORD reward you well for the way you treated me today" (v. 19).

Romans 12:17–21

"Do not repay anyone evil for evil. Be careful to do what is right in the eyes of everybody. If it is possible, as far as it depends on you, live at peace with everyone. Do not take revenge, my friends, but leave room for God's wrath, for it is written: 'It is mine to avenge; I will repay,' says the Lord. On the contrary: 'If your enemy is hungry, feed him; if he is thirsty, give him something to drink. In doing this, you will heap burning coals on his head.'"

James 1:19–21

"My dear brothers, take note of this: Everyone should be quick to listen, slow to speak and slow to become angry, for man's anger does not bring about the righteous life that God desires. Therefore, get rid of all moral filth and the evil that is so prevalent and humbly accept the word planted in you, which can save you."

▶ **15. Read aloud Romans 12:17-21 in the margin. Indicate how David and Saul illustrated these verses.**

_____

_____

_____

As far as we know, this was the first time Saul confessed publicly that he knew in his heart David was going to be the king of Israel. He only pleaded that when this happened, David would spare his life, his descendants, and his relatives (1 Sam. 24:20–21).

➡ David is a dynamic model to all of us who are tempted to retaliate by hurting someone who has hurt us. Though he was tempted to return evil for evil, he checked his behavior before he made an irreversible decision that would have haunted him the rest of his life.

His was a heart of restraint: restrained from revenge, restrained from seizing the kingdom, restrained from following popular opinion.

▶ **16. Read James 1:19–21 in the margin. James understood the need for restraint when he wrote, "Be quick to listen, slow to speak and slow to become angry." Why is this such good advice?**

_____

_____

_____

Let us hit the rewind button and go back to the cave. There lies helpless Saul. David squats down on his haunches, watching him. Words flow through David's mind. "See! I am giving your enemy into your hand . . . ." This was a soul-searching test for Yahweh's servant.

"The Anchor Slipped"

Then let us hit the fast-forward button and move into the next chapter. The Bible does not specifically say how much later this scene takes place, but one can be left muttering, "Oh, the difference a chapter can make." In one chapter, Saul is the man with a resentful heart, David's men have revengeful hearts, and David is the one showing restraint. In the next, David is beyond resentful and revengeful. He is on his way to commit murder!

David and his men were protecting shepherds in the southern part of the country. It was customary in those days that those who benefited from such efforts would at the time of shearing reward their protectors.

Nabal had received the benefit but would not pay anything in return. He was a wealthy man who chose instead to insult David, paying back good with evil.

▶ **17. David did good with hope of reward. Can you remember a time when you did good without hope of a reward?**

_____

_____

_____

The heart of restraint wavered. "Put on your swords!" he told his men (1 Sam. 25:13). This was his version of, "Mount up, we're going to ride." With 400 armed men, David went after Nabal. Insulted, he jumped to the attack.

Charles Swindoll provides good insights into this scene. He writes,

"The rays of each sunrise bring new opportunities to be taken and new choices to be made.

"Yet, while each day carries with it a certain aura of adventure and growth and the possibility of success, it also brings the painful possibility of failure. Though God's mercies are new every morning, so are Satan's schemes.

"Yesterday's victories may become today's temptations; the sin we shunned yesterday, we may embrace today.

"Sunday's unconditional love can turn to Monday's selfishness.

"A tender, forgiving heart can become punitive and tough.

"And a refusal to retaliate can turn to cold-blooded revenge."[5]

David's anchor slipped! For a brief moment his heart was far from God. But though his anchor slipped, it held.

Abigail, Nabal's wife, heard what was happening. She wasted no time in gathering food and hurrying to meet David. The man leading his fighters was confronted by a woman with wise words. He listened. Stopped cold in his tracks, David heard the wise counsel.

David's response to Abigail was immediate. What she said had reached the depths of his heart, from which his desire for revenge had sprung. "Praise be to the LORD, the God of Israel, who has sent you today to meet me," David told her. "May you be blessed for your good judgment and for keeping me from bloodshed this day and from avenging myself with my own hands" (1 Sam. 25:32–33).

Galatians 6:1–2

"Brothers, if someone is caught in a sin, you who are spiritual should restore him gently. But watch yourself, or you also may be tempted. Carry each other's burden, and in this way you will fulfill the law of Christ."

▶ **18. Abigail helped David do the right thing. Galatians 6:1–2 (in the margin) reminds us of our responsibility to do the same. What instruction is given in these verses?**

_____

_____

_____

What warning is given in these verses?

_____

_____

_____

This near disaster was good preparation for what lie ahead. Again in the next chapter, 1 Samuel 26, David has an opportunity to kill Saul but chooses to spare him.

Remember the quote of Kenneth Chafin? "When I study the Scriptures I try to find myself in the stories." David did not cave in to the temptation. His was not a heart of resentment or revenge but of restraint. Even when he wavered, he was still receptive to wise counsel.

We keep from caving in by learning from David's example. We keep from caving in by checking our hearts and following God's rules.

Small-Group Meeting 4

Opening Prayer

Begin your time together with prayer. Ask God to help you approach this lesson of David with an open heart. Be willing to let the Holy Spirit bring conviction and change. Pray that God will help you get rid of all resentment and the desire for revenge.

Building Relationships

Allow group members to share something from their journals, perhaps an especially meaningful verse that they noted during the past week, a prayer that was answered, or a blessing they received.

Reviewing the Lesson

1. The theme of this lesson is the restrained heart. What are some common situations where you are tempted to get back at someone?

2. What were the basic reasons for Saul's resentment of David (see Part 2 on page 53)?

3. Who encouraged David to kill Saul, and what did they quote to encourage him to do so?

4. David acted righteously. What four things demonstrate his righteousness in 1 Samuel 24:8–15?

5. Ask someone to retell the account of David and Nabal (1 Sam. 25:1–35).

6. Discuss why you think David so quickly changed in verse 32.

Applying the Truths to Life

Select interactive questions to discuss as a group. Be careful to choose ones that are for open discussion, since some are intended for personal reflection and are not for sharing with the group. Include some from each of the four parts of the lesson.

Questions to consider from this lesson include #6 (page 53), #8 (page 55), #11 (page 57), and #15 (page 60).

Ministering to One Another

Are you encouraging others to do right? Abigail kept David from an act of revenge. Similarly, there are times when we need to confront a person about something wrong in his or her life. We also ought to encourage those who are doing right. Think of someone who recently made a good decision. Plan to affirm that person for doing right.

Reaching Out to Others

If yours is an open group, did you set an empty chair in your circle? What will you do to fill it next time you meet? If yours is a closed group, begin discussing the possibility of a couple of people from your group leading others through this same study.

Closing Prayer Time

Go through your prayer sheets item by item and ask for an update. Following this, share new prayer requests. Remind the group of the importance of keeping confidences, and then pray together. These prayer times will help group members discover opportunities to minister to one another.

*F*orm or Function?
A Responsive Heart

2 Samuel 6

What is worship?

Billy Sunday used to say, "Going to church doesn't make a man a Christian any more than going to a garage makes him a car." A biblically correct understanding of salvation recognizes that it is not a matter of being in the right place but of having the right heart. Paul said, "For it is with your heart that you believe and are justified, and it is with your mouth that you confess and are saved" (Rom. 10:10).

Here is a fractured version of Sunday's quote: "Going to church doesn't make a Christian a worshiper any more than going to a ball game makes him a player." This is true for the same reason. Worship is not a matter of being in the right place but of having the right heart.

Going to a ball game can be quite similar to attending a church service. Both can have printed programs, ushers, uncomfortable seats, distractions, and performers to watch. It is readily agreeable that one can go a ball game but not play. In the same way, one can go to a worship service but not worship. Sadly, this is the experience for many people.

Sometimes we mistake the "art" of worship for the "heart" of worship. The "art" form of worship treats worship as if it were only a noun — a place or a thing. It is something attended, not something that is done.

When looking at the heart of worship, one realizes that it is a verb, something you do. That is the idea behind the Greek word for worship (*latreuo*), which means "to serve."

The real essence of worship is that it is a response. For the believer, it is the response to God in which that person declares by word and deed His worth.

Warren Wiersbe states it well: "Worship is the believer's response of all that he is—mind, emotions, will, and body—to all that God is and says and does. This response has its mystical side in subjective experience, and its practical side in objective obedience to God's revealed truth. It is a loving response that is balanced by the fear of the Lord, and it is a deepening response as the believer comes to know God better."[1]

> Worship is a response to God, a declaration by word and deed of His worth.

If we truly desire to worship biblically, we determine what the biblical elements of worship are and seek to bring those into our lives, corporately (as a church) and personally.

▶ **1. The subject of worship has been given much attention recently. Is it clear in your mind what it is? Take the two parts of Wiersbe's definition: the believer and God. Restate his definition by choosing your own words and phrases for each of the following. Make it very personal. For the first part, use the first-person singular, as in "my" (see example below).**

The believer's

a. mind

My worship is not mindless. I think about the things I have learned of God from the Bible.

b. emotions

_____

c. will

_____

d. body

_____

In regard to God

a. all that He is

_____

b. says

_____

c. does

_____

David had a heart that responded to all that God is, says, and does. He did so with all that he was—mind, emotions, will, and body. His responsive heart teaches us that the heart anchored close to God is responsive to God.

PART 1: Interacting with the Scripture

Reading/Hearing God's Word

► 2. Using your Bible, read or listen to the passages of Scripture in the margin. As you begin, ask God to speak to you through His Word. Watch for verses or ideas that are especially meaningful to you today. Once you finish reading, check the box indicating the passage(s) you read.

Meditating on God's Word

► 3. Write a brief summary of a meaningful verse or idea you noticed.

_____

_____

_____

Understanding God's Word

► 4. Read again the focal passage for this week's lesson (2 Sam. 6:12–15) in the margin. Underline any key phrases or words that seem especially meaningful to you.

► 5. Look back at this passage. Circle a key word or phrase that you would like to understand or experience more fully.

Looking through the Scripture to God

 Now pause to pray, asking God to help you consider your worship. Is it merely a form, a service attended, or is it a response to Him? Pray that God will help you take that heart attitude to church on Sunday, responding to all that He is, says, and does.

PART 2: David's Desire

The scene in 2 Samuel 6 is not one of spiritual health. Israel's condition had declined during Saul's reign. Charles Swindoll summarizes the situation this way: "Israel had become spiritually malnourished under Saul's reign. The tabernacle had deteriorated, its furnishings had been scattered, and the worship itself had become virtually meaningless. Since God's presence was associated with the tabernacle furnishings, the people of Israel no longer felt His nearness. As Israel's new king, David wanted to reestablish the center of worship—to renew his people's fear of God and fatten their spiritual fervor."[2]

Read or Listen to:

☐ 2 Samuel 6:1–23

☐ Psalm 19

☐ Psalm 29

☐ Psalm 65

2 Samuel 6:12-15

"Now King David was told, 'The LORD has blessed the household of Obed-Edom and everything he has, because of the ark of God.' So David went down and brought up the ark of God from the house of Obed-Edom to the City of David with rejoicing. When those who were carrying the ark of the LORD had taken six steps, he sacrificed a bull and a fattened calf. David, wearing a linen ephod, danced before the LORD with all his might, while he and the entire house of Israel brought up the ark of the LORD with shouts and the sound of trumpets."

▶ **6. Worship is not limited to a place or a time. Which of the following are places where you worship? Note what it is like for you to worship in these places.**

☐ church

_____

☐ a quiet place at home

_____

☐ a favorite outdoor spot

_____

☐ a hiking trail or bike path

_____

☐ a car commuting to work

_____

☐ other

_____

David desired to bring the ark of God to Jerusalem. The ark was a chest made of acacia wood, gold-plated inside and out, and rimmed with a border of gold. It was three and three-quarters feet long, two and a half feet wide, and two and one-quarter feet high. Its pure gold lid—the mercy seat—held two cherubs of hammered gold, with wings outstretched over the cover. The ark held only three objects: a golden jar containing manna, Aaron's rod, and the Ten Commandments (Heb. 9:4).

But the ark was much more than a historic relic to Israel. It represented the dwelling place of God.

The ark was in the home of Abinadab, about 20 miles west of Jerusalem, where it had been since the Philistines returned it to Israel (1 Sam. 6–7). Moving the ark was both a major and a majestic project. Thirty thousand men were involved in the procession (2 Sam. 6:1). The celebration must have been phenomenal, as "David and the whole house of Israel were celebrating with all their might before the LORD" (v. 5).

> **To Israel, the ark represented the dwelling place of God.**

▶ **7. Describe how this celebration fits various aspects of the definition of worship.**

_____

_____

_____

David wanted to bring the ark of God to the newly occupied city of Jerusalem. Sadly, it did not stay a time of rejoicing but became one of judgment. David did the right thing but in the wrong way. The first mistake he made was asking for help from the wrong people. He went to the military leaders, not the priests, for assistance in moving the ark (1 Chron. 13:1).

God had given instructions to the Levites that they were the only ones who were to move the ark. David should have asked them, since they were the ones chosen by God to lead the nation in its worship.

▶ **8. To whom do people go for advice or help?**

_____

_____

To whom should God's people go for advice or help?

_____

_____

The second mistake David made was in how the ark was moved. When God instructed Moses in fashioning the ark, it was designed to be carried on poles (Ex. 37:3–5), not in a cart. Verses 6–9 in 2 Samuel 6 describe the disaster that occurred. This incident is a vivid illustration that joy can change to fear when we disobey God.

The Bible does not gloss over the fact that David's disobedience brought disaster. But it also gives insight into David's heart. He desired to worship God. His was a heart that responded to God.

PART 3: David Responded to God

With Rejoicing (2 Sam. 6:5)

The nation joined with David in a time of rejoicing. It was a whole-hearted celebration of God. They used the musical instruments of their day—harps, lyres, tambourines, sistrums, and cymbals—to praise their Lord.

Philippians 4:4

"Rejoice in the Lord always. I will say it again: Rejoice!"

▶ **9. Do you rejoice? List some verses, such as Philippians 4:4 (in the margin), that especially help you rejoice or remind you of the joy of the Lord.**

_____

_____

What are some past experiences of God's blessing that brought you joy?

_____

_____

As David led the procession to Jerusalem, his response to God was one of rejoicing. Yet we must realize that even in rejoicing we need to have reverence for God.

With Reverence (2 Sam. 6:8–11)

David's reaction to the judgment of God was twofold. First, he was angry. That was a normal reaction considering what he was trying to do and how much effort he had put into it. But the right reaction quickly followed: "David was afraid of the LORD that day" (v. 9).

The fear of God is a missing and misunderstood element today. He is approachable through Jesus. It is our privilege to enter into His presence at any time—whereas in David's day, access to the Holy Place was limited to the priests. We also have God's Word, the Bible, which is a blessing not everyone in the world can enjoy. But just as "familiarity breeds contempt," sometimes Christians get so accustomed to the things of God that our reverential awe of Him diminishes. It's as if we've lost our sense of awe of our Creator.

► 10. Is God awesome to you? In what ways?

_____

_____

What reminds you that He is awesome?

_____

_____

David's fear of God manifested itself not in cowering but in making certain that he moved the ark correctly this time. In 1 Chronicles 15 it is noted that he then asked the right people, the Levites, to move the ark.

Obedience is a response. What a person respects he will obey.

Rejoicing and reverence are brought together in Psalm 95 (in the margin). Verses 1–5 emphasize singing and shouting aloud. Verses 6–7 call the worshiper to bow down before the Lord our Maker. Flowing out of these two calls to worship is a call to revival (vv. 8–11).

► 11. **Which of the following are proper responses to God's correction?**

☐ fear of God   ☐ running from God

☐ repentance   ☐ ignoring the correction

☐ understanding what was wrong

Psalm 95

"Come, let us sing for joy to the LORD; let us shout aloud to the Rock of our salvation. Let us come before him with thanksgiving and extol him with music and song.

"For the LORD is the great God, the great King above all gods. In his hand are the depths of the earth, and the mountain peaks belong to him. The sea is his, for he made it, and his hands formed the dry land.

"Come, let us bow down in worship, let us kneel before the LORD our Maker; for he is our God and we are the people of his pasture, the flock under his care.

"Today, if you hear his voice, do not harden your hearts as you did at Meribah, as you did that day at Massah in the desert, where your fathers tested and tried me, though they had seen what I did. For forty years I was angry with that generation; I said, 'They are a people whose hearts go astray and they have not known my ways.' So I declared an oath in my anger, 'They shall never enter my rest.'"

With Renewed Rejoicing (2 Sam. 6:12)

God dealt with David decisively. David's heart responded to God, even when corrected by Him. Perhaps one of the greatest challenges to our hearts is when we realize that God is not pleased with us. Changing our attitudes and/or actions so as to return to God's favor is truly the sign of a heart that worships God for what He is.

David's worship here is one of joy. He rejoiced because of the blessing of God. The sacrifices he offered were offerings of worship. It is interesting to note that God's rebuke did not drive David away but renewed his rejoicing.

His enthusiastic worship of God is undeniable, though it drew the criticism of his wife because it was so exuberant.

David danced before the Lord (v.14). This is a scene of a worshiper of the true God who learned to worship Him in the right way. His heart was anchored close to God and he rejoiced with reverent worship.

PART 4: David's Psalms

One day while tending his father's sheep, David composed some beautiful words as he led the flock through green pastures and by still pools of fresh water. As he faithfully protected them from wild animals in secluded valleys and poured oil on their wounds, David saw a parallel between himself and God, his divine Shepherd. Inspired both by his pastoral experience and the Holy Spirit, he wrote one of the most beautiful psalms ever penned:

► **12. Read Psalm 23 slowly and aloud. It is easy to skim familiar verses, so force yourself to thoroughly read and meditate on this and the other passages quoted in the remainder of this lesson.**

Psalm 23

The LORD is my shepherd, I shall not be in want.
    He makes me lie down in green pastures,
he leads me beside quiet waters,
    he restores my soul.
He guides me in paths of righteousness
    for his name's sake.
Even though I walk
    through the valley of the shadow of death,
I will fear no evil,
    for you are with me;
your rod and your staff,
    they comfort me.

You prepare a table before me
    in the presence of my enemies.
You anoint my head with oil;
    my cup overflows.
Surely goodness and love will follow me
    all the days of my life,
and I will dwell in the house of the LORD
    forever.

These familiar verses give insight into the responsive heart of David. To be a man *after* God's own heart required him to have a heart *for* God. Even in his ordinary, everyday life as a shepherd, David worshiped God.

▶ **13. What reminds you of God? Look at the ordinary things of your life and take note of the evidences of God in them. This list can include the beauty of creation, the changing of the seasons in accordance with His promise, the love of family members, and so on.**

_____

_____

_____

_____

Every psalm David wrote gives us fascinating insights into his ideas, attitudes, and feelings toward God. Following are some selective highlights from his psalms that focus on his references to the heart.

The Omnipotent Creator

"The heavens declare." Several of David's psalms focus on God's creative power. David was an outdoorsman, a man who spent many hours—day and night—absorbing the splendor, beauty, and mysteries of nature. Inspired by God's Spirit, he expressed his thoughts in poetry. Psalm 19, for example, reveals David's convictions and feelings about the firmament, particularly the sun in its journey across space:

Psalm 19:1–6
The heavens declare the glory of God;
    the skies proclaim the work of his hands.
Day after day they pour forth speech;
    night after night they display knowledge.

There is no speech or language
    where their voice is not heard.
Their voice goes out into all the earth,
    their words to the ends of the world.

In the heavens he has pitched a tent for the sun,
    which is like a bridegroom coming forth from his pavilion,
    like a champion rejoicing to run his course.
It rises at one end of the heavens
    and makes its circuit to the other;
    nothing is hidden from its heat.

▶ **14. "Field trip time!" Remember how much you enjoyed hearing those words in school? Why not take a field trip now? Go outside and look up. The heavens declare the glory of God. Don't miss their message.**

"The voice of the LORD." David's view of God's creative power in nature often generated praise, thanksgiving, and worship in his heart. In Psalm 29 he wrote about a storm. While most of us understandably focus on our fears and anxieties in the midst of this kind of natural turbulence, David's heart focused on God. Though he, too, probably experienced fear, what he observed and felt reflected the "voice of the LORD":

Psalm 29:3–9
The voice of the LORD is over the waters;
    the God of glory thunders,
    the LORD thunders over the mighty waters.
The voice of the LORD is powerful;
    the voice of the LORD is majestic.
The voice of the LORD breaks the cedars;
    the LORD breaks in pieces the cedars of Lebanon.
He makes Lebanon skip like a calf,
    Sirion like a young wild ox.
The voice of the LORD strikes
    with flashes of lightning.
The voice of the LORD shakes the desert;
    the LORD shakes the Desert of Kadesh.
The voice of the LORD twists the oaks
    and strips the forests bare.
And in his temple all cry, "Glory!"

"They shout for joy." David also was impressed with the four seasons and God's provisions to cause the earth to produce all kinds of vegetation to sustain both mankind and animals, as this psalm reveals:

Psalm 65:9–13

You care for the land and water it;
    you enrich it abundantly.
The streams of God are filled with water
      to provide the people with grain,
      for so you have ordained it.
You drench its furrows
      and level its ridges;
you soften it with showers
      and bless its crops.
You crown the year with your bounty,
      and your carts overflow with abundance.
The grasslands of the desert overflow;
      the hills are clothed with gladness.
The meadows are covered with flocks
      and the valleys are mantled with grain;
      they shout for joy and sing.

▶ **15. What is your favorite season of the year and why?**

_____

_____

_____

What does God do at that time of the year that is a special blessing to you?

_____

_____

_____

The Omniscient God

"Such knowledge is too wonderful for me." David understood that God knew everything about him—every detail of his heart and his actions at any given moment. This is apparent in the opening verses of Psalm 139:

Psalm 139:1–6

O LORD, you have searched me
    and you know me.
You know when I sit down and when I rise;
    you perceive my thoughts from afar.
You discern my going out and my lying down;
    you are familiar with all my ways.
Before a word is on my tongue
    you know it completely, O LORD.

You hem me in—behind and before;
    you have laid your hand upon me.
Such knowledge is too wonderful for me,
    too lofty for me to attain.

 Pause for a moment of silence here. Realize that God knows you intimately! He knows all about you. That awesome truth should make you rejoice. Pray right now, praising God for His omniscience.

The Omnipresent Spirit

"Where can I flee from your presence?" David not only viewed God as omnipotent (all-powerful) and omniscient (all-knowing), but also as omnipresent. In other words, God was everywhere David went—to guide him, to protect him, to comfort him, and to search out his heart:

Psalm 139:7–12

Where can I go from your Spirit?
    Where can I flee from your presence?
If I go up to the heavens, you are there;
    if I make my bed in the depths, you are there.
If I rise on the wings of the dawn,
    if I settle on the far side of the sea,
even there your hand will guide me,
    your right hand will hold me fast.

If I say, "Surely the darkness will hide me
    and the light become night around me,"
even the darkness will not be dark to you;
    the night will shine like the day,
    for darkness is as light to you.

► **16.** This psalm gives another opportunity to develop a responsive heart. Worship God. He is present everywhere right now. Think about what that means for you. You are never alone, never away, never apart from His presence. What you do not want to be is never aware of His presence!

The God of Loving Concern

"What is man that you are mindful of him?" If God was so involved in preserving what He had created in nature, how much more was He concerned for all mankind! David understood this great truth. Furthermore, the fact that the Lord gave human beings a certain degree of authority and control over His natural creation overwhelmed David, as he expressed in Psalm 8:

Psalm 8:3–9
When I consider your heavens,
 the work of your fingers,
the moon and the stars,
 which you have set in place,
what is man that you are mindful of him?
 the son of man that you care for him?
You made him a little lower than the heavenly beings
 and crowned him with glory and honor.

You made him ruler over the works of your hands;
 you put everything under his feet:
all flocks and herds,
 and the beasts of the field,
the birds of the air,
 and the fish of the sea,
 all that swim the paths of the seas.

O LORD, our Lord,
 how majestic is your name in all the earth!

 Pray, thanking God that He cares for you.

The God of Love

"Your love . . . your faithfulness . . . your righteousness." The vastness of the universe also reminded David of God's personal attributes, as he expressed in this psalm:

Psalm 36:5–6

Your love, O LORD, reaches to the heavens,
    your faithfulness to the skies.
Your righteousness is like the mighty mountains,
    your justice like the great deep.
O LORD, you preserve both man and beast.

Many other psalms reveal David's view of God. But these few demonstrate dramatically why David was a man after God's heart. He responded to all that God is and does with all that he was.

▶ **17. Is your heart a responsive heart, or was this emphasis on worship too emotional for you? Consider in closing these questions:**

What is your view of God? Is it anything like David's?

_____

_____

_____

Is your heart responsive or non-responsive? A heart for God responds to all that He is, says, and does. Give an example of something from the Bible that causes you to respond with joy/awe/thankfulness.

_____

_____

_____

Do you put voice to your worship? This is done in prayer, praise, and testimony. How is your worship evident to others in your words and life?

_____

_____

_____

Small-Group Meeting 5

Opening Prayer

As you begin your time together pray, with special emphasis on worship. Ask God to help you approach this lesson on David with a quiet heart. Pray that your focus in this meeting will be totally on God and His Word.

Building Relationships

Allow time for every member to share one thing for which they praise God.

Reviewing the Lesson

1. The theme of this lesson is the responsive heart. Ask members to talk about a recent worship service that affected them emotionally. What was said or done in the service (e.g., special music, a testimony) that really moved them?

2. What is Warren Wiersbe's definition of worship (see page 65)?

3. Why was the ark in the home of Abinadab (1 Sam. 6:1–7:2)?

4. Why was God angry with Uzzah (2 Sam. 6:7)?

5. In what two ways did David react to God's judgment (2 Sam. 6:8–11)?

6. What did David do that allowed him finally to move the ark to Jerusalem (2 Sam. 6:12; 1 Chron. 15:11–15)?

Applying the Truths to Life

Select interactive questions to discuss as a group. Be careful to choose ones that are for open discussion, since some are intended for personal reflection and are not for sharing with the group. Include some from each of the four parts of the lesson. In addition, allow time to read several of the psalms from this lesson as suggested in the next paragraph. To prepare for that exercise, discuss #7 (page 68), #9 (page 69), #10 (page 70), and #13 (page 72).

Next, lead the group in a time of worship. Read several of the psalms aloud, slowly. After each reading, ask the group to pray, thanking God for the special things that the psalm says about Him. Worshiping God by responding to what His Word says about Him can be a very meaningful time of applying the truths to life.

Ministering to One Another

Review activities that individuals or the group as a whole has done to encourage one another. This study has only one more lesson. Challenge the group not to stop helping others when the study is done.

Reaching Out to Others

If yours is an open group, did you set an empty chair in your circle? The final lesson is a very important one. It is not too late to invite someone. What will you do to fill it next time you meet? If your group is a closed group, ask members how serious some of them might be about leading another group through this study.

Closing Prayer Time

Looking at your prayer sheets, ask for an update on each item. Then allow members time to mention new prayer requests. Remind everyone of the importance of keeping confidences, and pray as a group for the needs that are mentioned.

The Cry of a Broken Spirit
A Repentant Heart

Psalm 51

The Bible teaches us how to live not just by giving us principles but also by relating true stories of real people. Some of these are "spiritual success stories," but others are accounts of people's failures.

Remember this quotation by the late Dr. Alan Redpath from Lesson 3? "I find it tremendously comforting that the Bible never flatters its heroes. It tells the truth about them no matter how unpleasant it may be, so that in considering what is taking place in the shaping of their character we have available all the facts clearly that we may study them."

With that in mind, our attention in this lesson is focused on a sad scene from the life of David, one of tragic moral failure. Nearly 20 years after David first occupied the throne, he committed one of the greatest sins of his life.

The lessons that can be learned from David's involvement with Bathsheba are numerous. Among them is what we learn about the heart of the man after God's own heart. There is no denying the sins that are recorded in 2 Samuel 11 and their consequences. In this study, however, we focus on the sinner's heart. David had a repentant heart.

Exodus 20:13, 15–16

"'You shall not murder. . . . You shall not steal. You shall not give false testimony against your neighbor.'"

▶ 1. Look carefully at 2 Samuel 11, and then read Exodus 20:13, 15–16 in the margin. List the sins that are found in this account of David and Bathsheba.

_____

_____

_____

James 1:13–15

"When tempted, no one should say, 'God is tempting me.' For God cannot be tempted by evil, nor does he tempt anyone; but each one is tempted when, by his own evil desire, he is dragged away and enticed. Then, after desire has conceived, it gives birth to sin; and sin, when it is full-grown, gives birth to death."

1 Corinthians 9:27

"I beat my body and make it my slave so that after I have preached to others, I myself will not be disqualified for the prize."

Read or Listen to:

☐ 2 Samuel 11

☐ 2 Samuel 12:1–25

☐ Psalm 51

☐ Matthew 5:28

☐ 1 John 1:9

▶ 2. Read James 1:13–15 in the margin. What are the steps James describes that lead from temptation to death?

a. _____

b. _____

c. _____

The believer who seeks to be close to God will at times fail. But the heart that is anchored close to God will be repentant. Without repentance, sin has a negative effect on a person's relationship with God. The heart will not be as close to Him as it once was.

Read 1 Corinthians 9:27 in the margin. It is remarkable to see how concerned Paul was about not becoming a castaway. Are you as concerned? Pray that God will help you see the importance of purity in the lives of all believers. Ask that He will help you understand how vital it is in the lives of those who serve Him. We should desire to be useable vessels for the Master. And we should dread that we might not be useable because of moral failure.

PART 1: Interacting with the Scripture

Reading/Hearing God's Word

▶ 3. Using your Bible, read or listen to the passages of Scripture in the margin. As you begin, ask God to speak to you through His Word. Watch for verses or ideas that are especially meaningful to you today. Once you finish reading, check the box indicating the passage(s) you read.

Meditating on God's Word

▶ 4. Write a brief summary of a meaningful verse or idea you noticed.

_____

_____

_____

Psalm 51:1–12

"Have mercy on me, O God, according to your unfailing love; according to your great compassion blot out my transgressions. Wash away all my iniquity and cleanse me from my sin.

"For I know my transgressions, and my sin is always before me. Against you, you only, have I sinned and done what is evil in your sight, so that you are proved right when you speak and justified when you judge. Surely I was sinful at birth, sinful from the time my mother conceived me. Surely you desire truth in the inner parts; you teach me wisdom in the inmost place.

"Cleanse me with hyssop, and I will be clean; wash me, and I will be whiter than snow.

"Let me hear joy and gladness; let the bones you have crushed rejoice. Hide your face from my sins and blot out all my iniquity.

"Create in me a pure heart, O God, and renew a steadfast spirit within me. Do not cast me from your presence or take your Holy Spirit from me. Restore to me the joy of your salvation and grant me a willing spirit, to sustain me."

Understanding God's Word

▶ 5. Read again the focal passage for this week's lesson (Ps. 51:1–12) in the margin. Underline any key phrases or words that seem especially meaningful to you.

▶ 6. Look back through the words and phrases you underlined. Circle one that you would like to understand or experience more fully.

Looking through the Scripture to God

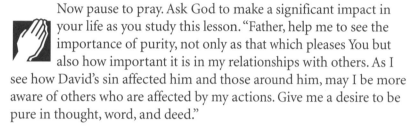

Now pause to pray. Ask God to make a significant impact in your life as you study this lesson. "Father, help me to see the importance of purity, not only as that which pleases You but also how important it is in my relationships with others. As I see how David's sin affected him and those around him, may I be more aware of others who are affected by my actions. Give me a desire to be pure in thought, word, and deed."

PART 2: How It Happened (2 Sam. 11:1–4)

David had been actively involved in leading the armies of Israel against their enemies. Through his leadership, they had defeated nearly everyone who was a threat to their national security. At this point in his life, David was relatively free from military responsibility. He gladly turned over his military role to Joab, his faithful commander, who could easily handle any skirmishes against the enemies of Israel.

No one would deny that David had earned the right to relax and enjoy his position as king. He was now about 50 years old, having spent many of those years in active duty as a warrior on the front lines. He had paid his dues.

▶ 7. Once again, idle time leads to trouble. In Lesson 4, we saw that Saul pursued David when he had time on his hands. What principle do these situations teach you regarding how you use your free time?

_____

_____

_____

One afternoon while David was lying down to rest, he couldn't sleep. He arose from his bed and went out on the roof of his house—a vantage point that gave him a bird's-eye view of most of Jerusalem. As he walked about viewing the city, perhaps contemplating his success as king, he couldn't help noticing a woman who was bathing on a nearby rooftop. The Bible states that she was "very beautiful" (v. 2). The glance became a gaze. David quickly responded to what he saw. He found out who she was, sent for her, and committed adultery.

▶ 8. **Think about how many opportunities to "glance" at something we shouldn't see surround us on a daily basis. In what situations might you find it easy to let your glance become a gaze?**

_____

_____

_____

Some Bible scholars believe Bathsheba may have been trying to seduce David. This, of course, is feasible since she no doubt had noticed the king on many occasions strolling on his rooftop. Perhaps she was purposely trying to attract his attention.

▶ 9. **(For women especially.) Do you realize that men are stimulated visually? As you consider your appearance and dress, ask yourself these questions:**

a. Do I dress modestly?

_____

b. Do I try to entice men by the way I dress?

_____

c. Am I concerned about how my appearance could be a toying with sin?

_____

Nevertheless, what David did is inexcusable. He openly violated God's law.

PART 3: David's Schemes (2 Sam. 11:5–27)

In David's mind the event was over, but it wasn't. Bathsheba conceived his child (v. 5).

Had David been just another of the pagan kings who ruled at that time, he could have solved the problem quickly and easily. He simply could have taken Bathsheba into his own household, not caring what happened to her husband. Or he could have ignored her plight. Since a king was considered sovereign by his people, he could do anything he wanted. He was above the law.

Romans 12:1–2

"Therefore, I urge you, brothers, in view of God's mercy, to offer your bodies as living sacrifices, holy and pleasing to God—this is your spiritual act of worship. Do not conform any longer to the pattern of this world, but be transformed by the renewing of your mind. Then you will be able to test and approve what God's will is—his good, pleasing and perfect will."

▶ **10. Read Romans 12:1–2 in the margin. In what way did David not conform to the world?**

_____

_____

_____

As you compare David's actions with the world today, in what ways did he conform?

_____

_____

_____

For personal reflection, in what ways do you or do you not conform to the world?

_____

_____

_____

David had been anointed by God. He served a Lawgiver far superior to himself—One who had thundered from Mount Sinai many years before: "You shall not commit adultery. . . . You shall not covet your neighbor's house; you shall not covet your neighbor's wife, or his manservant or maidservant, his ox or donkey, or anything that belongs to your neighbor" (Ex. 20:14,17).

The king of Israel had sinned against his own King. Worse, David regressed to his old pattern of behavior and refused to acknowledge his sin. In fact, he may have talked himself into believing he was above God's law as king. Still, he knew he was facing a serious crisis, and he attempted to solve the problem all by himself. But as always happens in situations like this, he only became more entangled in his web of wrongdoing.

David's First Scheme

David first attempted to extricate himself from this predicament with the most logical idea he could think of. *I'll send for Uriah, Bathsheba's husband,* he thought. *I'll make him believe that I've sent for him to find out the welfare of Joab and the state of war. Then I'll give him some time off to spend with his wife. He'll never know the child is mine* (see 2 Sam. 11:6–8).

Genesis 3:12

"The man said, 'The woman you put here with me—she gave me some fruit from the tree, and I ate it.'"

▶ **11. This is what could be called "The Genesis 3 Defense." Adam told the Lord that he sinned because of the woman God had given him (see Gen. 3:12 in the margin). He tried to get the focus off of** his problem and onto someone else—in that instance, Eve, his wife. In a similar way, David tried to make it look like the child was Uriah's. Can you think of some hypothetical situations in which someone would try to get someone else to take the blame?

Thus David reasoned, and thus he acted. This sounds like the David we met in the land of the Philistines 20 years earlier. One sin led to another then—now he was giving a repeat performance. Circumstances were different, but the spiritual dynamics were the same. If we don't admit our sin, confess it, and seek forgiveness, we'll try to cover it up. This was David's plan.

To David's surprise, his simple, logical scheme didn't work. His great wisdom that had defeated armies could not deliver him from this self-imposed predicament. Uriah would not go home—which should have brought humiliating shame to David's heart. In fact, Uriah "slept at the entrance to the palace with all his master's servants" (v. 9). He was so loyal to David and his fellow soldiers who were camping in the open battlefield that he would not allow himself the indulgence of staying in the comforts of his own home, enjoying his wife's companionship.

David's Second Scheme

David next devised a plan to blur Uriah's thinking and dull his sensitive spirit. He purposely got Uriah drunk, hoping he would stumble on home and forget his military responsibilities—at least for one evening.

▶ 12. Which of the following are ways that people try to "blur" thinking?

☐ using pious words or statements

☐ quoting Bible verses out of context

☐ citing examples that seem to be the same but aren't

☐ using confused logic

☐ other _____

But again David's strategy failed. Even in his drunken stupor, Uriah would not go home. He stayed in the king's court and slept in the servants' quarters (v. 13).

By this time David was terribly frustrated. What was he going to do? He was both scared and angry—two emotions that frequently are found in a guilty heart.

David's Third Scheme

In his state of emotional turmoil, David made an incredible decision, especially in view of his personal relationship with God. He decided to have Uriah killed "legitimately"—that is, in battle. David would then be free, at least in the eyes of Israel, to take Bathsheba as one of his wives. No one except the cooperating parties would know.

David wrote a letter to his commanding officer, ironically sending it via Uriah. He instructed Joab to send Uriah to the front lines. When the battle was most intense, the general was to withdraw protection from Uriah and allow him to go it alone.

What makes this scheme so diabolical is that David knew Uriah would not retreat. He was too loyal! He had already proved that point when the first two schemes failed. David actually used Uriah's commitment to him as the king of Israel in order to take his life.

As the world knows, the scheme worked. Uriah fell in battle. When word came of his death, and after the time of mourning, David brought Bathsheba "to his house, and she became his wife" (v. 27). As far as David was concerned, he was "home free."

Again, if David had been a pagan king, life would have gone on as usual. But David was God's anointed. Consequently, we read that "the thing David had done displeased the LORD" (v. 27). Not only did he violate God's law by committing adultery, but in his efforts to cover up his sin, he lied, stole what did not belong to him, and committed murder. All of these acts violated specific laws God had issued to Moses as part of the Ten Commandments.

Deuteronomy 17:17

"'[The king] must not take many wives, or his heart will be led astray. He must not accumulate large amounts of silver and gold.'"

▶ **13. Is one ever completely home free when he has sinned? Read Deuteronomy 17:17 in the margin. David violated this stipulation and his sin had a negative effect. Note the importance of obeying all that God says to do.**

_____

_____

_____

A man after God's own heart? It sounds impossible at this point to think that we can learn how to anchor our hearts close to God by looking at David—a man who married the widow of a loyal subject whose death he had ordered.

Proverbs 27:17

"As iron sharpens iron, so one man sharpens another."

▶ **14. Read the following verses (in the margin) and write down what they say about how God uses others in our life.**

Proverbs 27:17

_____

_____

Matthew 18:15–17

"'If your brother sins against you, go and show him his fault, just between the two of you. If he listens to you, you have won your brother over. But if he will not listen, take one or two others along, so that "every matter may be established by the testimony of two or three witnesses." If he refuses to listen to them, tell it to the church; and if he refuses to listen even to the church, treat him as you would a pagan or a tax collector.'"

Galatians 6:1–2

"Brothers, if someone is caught in a sin, you who are spiritual should restore him gently. But watch yourself, or you also may be tempted. Carry each other's burdens, and in this way you will fulfill the law of Christ."

Leviticus 20:10

"'If a man commits adultery with another man's wife—with the wife of his neighbor—both the adulterer and the adulteress must be put to death.'"

Leviticus 24:17

"'If anyone takes the life of a human being, he must be put to death.'"

Matthew 18:15–17

_____

_____

Galatians 6:1–2

_____

_____

For nearly a year David was able to cover his sin. Then the Lord sent Nathan the prophet to see the king and tell him a story about a rich man who stole from a poor man (2 Sam. 12:1–4).

▶ 15. Read Leviticus 20:10 and 24:17 in the margin. According to these verses, what did David deserve?

_____

_____

▶ 16. David listened to Nathan. God's messenger brought the king's need for repentance to the forefront of his life. God still has messengers who speak His Word to us. He has given to the church pastor-teachers. God intends them to carry His message to His people. Which of the following do you do during a sermon?

☐ wait patiently for it to end

☐ plan the rest of the day

☐ critique the service

☐ listen

☐ take notes

☐ take it to heart

Nathan moved from storytelling to interpretation—and confrontation! He pulled David's mask from his blinded eyes so he could see his self-deception. "You are the man!" (2 Sam. 12:7).

His words plunged like a knife into David's heart! His world of greatness suddenly crumbled around him as judgment was pronounced and he saw himself for what he was—an adulterer, a liar, a thief, and a murderer.

PART 4: The Repentant Heart (2 Sam. 12:1–14; Ps. 51)

Then David confessed to Nathan, "I have sinned against the LORD" (2 Sam. 12:13). To learn how to anchor our hearts close to God, we can look at David, a man with a repentant heart.

After his confrontation with Nathan, the king penned perhaps one of his most moving psalms. Psalm 51 is laced with an attitude of genuine repentance. In this psalm we learn the characteristics of a repentant heart. Listen to his words. Hear the cry of his broken spirit, and you will know the heart of a man truly sorry for his sin.

▶ **17. Read aloud Psalm 51:1–6.**

Have mercy on me, O God,
    according to your unfailing love;
according to your great compassion
    blot out my transgressions.
Wash away all my iniquity
    and cleanse me from my sin.

For I know my transgressions,
    and my sin is always before me.
Against you, you only, have I sinned
    and done what is evil in your sight,
so that you are proved right when you speak
    and justified when you judge.
Surely I was sinful at birth,
    sinful from the time my mother conceived me.
Surely you desire truth in the inner parts;
    you teach me wisdom in the inmost place.

A Repentant Heart Confesses (vv. 1–6)

When David wrote this psalm, he was well past the cover-up. Now he acknowledges his wrongdoing in a way that expresses the seriousness of sin. This is done by the use of three different words for wrongdoing: *transgressions, iniquity,* and *sin.* The same literary device is found in Psalm 32.

A *transgression (pesha)* is nothing less than rebellion. The use of this word indicates that David acknowledged his actions as a rebellion against God.

The next word for wrongdoing is *iniquity (hawon).* This connotes the perverting and twisting of moral standards. God has established His law, upon which morality is based. To commit iniquity, to be immoral, is to pervert and twist that standard. The application of this word to David's sexual immorality is obvious.

When David used the Hebrew word (*chatta'th*) translated as "sin," he directed the reader's attention to how he had missed the mark. God has set for us a goal to be holy as He is holy (1 Pet. 1:16). David had missed the mark.

Each of these words is a strong term. Combined, they intensify the seriousness of sin.

There is no redefining of words here. Today, some people try to make even the word *is* mean something other than it is. Not so with David. A repentant heart allows no room for evasive words. The godly cry out, readily confessing their sin.

In the quiet of your heart, answer this question: Is there something you need to confess to God? To your spouse? Pause for a moment of prayer, then . . .

▶ **18. Read aloud Psalm 51:7–9.**

> Cleanse me with hyssop, and I will be clean;
> > wash me, and I will be whiter than snow.
> Let me hear joy and gladness;
> > let the bones you have crushed rejoice.
> Hide your face from my sins
> > and blot out all my iniquity.

A Repentant Heart Desires Cleansing (vv. 7–9)

David desired that his sin would be forgiven, that the dirtiness of his life would be cleansed. This desire flowed out of a heart that was deeply aware of its sin, of having offended God, and of being in desperate need of His grace.

▶ **19. Think of something you cleaned recently. Explain why cleaning is such a good illustration of what it means to repent and ask for forgiveness.**

_____

_____

_____

Nothing in himself could accomplish this. David's cry to God was for the cleansing that would return to him both health and happiness.

► **20. Read aloud Psalm 51:10–17.**

Create in me a pure heart, O God,
    and renew a steadfast spirit within me.
Do not cast me from your presence
    or take your Holy Spirit from me.
Restore to me the joy of your salvation
    and grant me a willing spirit, to sustain me.

Then I will teach transgressors your ways,
    and sinners will turn back to you.
Save me from bloodguilt, O God,
    the God who saves me,
    and my tongue will sing of your righteousness.
O Lord, open my lips,
    and my mouth will declare your praise.
You do not delight in sacrifice, or I would bring it;
    you do not take pleasure in burnt offerings.
The sacrifices of God are a broken spirit;
    a broken and contrite heart,
    O God, you will not despise.

A Repentant Heart Determines to Change (vv. 10–17)

Repentance is more than admitting that one has done wrong. A person can be caught in the act and acknowledge the deed, but still not repent. The repentance God desires is also more than a sorrow for what was done. When Judas saw Jesus condemned, the King James Version translates Matthew 27:3 with the phrase, "[he] repented himself." Other versions carefully delineate the Greek word used here (*metamellomai*) from the other one translated "repented" (*metanoew*). In this passage the word means that Judas felt sorrow but that he did not truly repent.

The repentance that God desires is one that brings about change. The Greek word for this kind of repentance, along with the word used in Matthew 27, is found in 2 Corinthians 7:8–10. Paul wrote, "Even if I caused you sorrow . . ." (v. 8). This is the word from Matthew 27 (*metamellomai*). In the next verse the word implying change (*metanoew*) is used. Paul is glad that the sorrow led them to repentance.

► **21. If God is working in your life regarding a sin, which is your response—sorrow or change? Perhaps on a separate sheet of paper, write what steps you need to take in order to change. Be specific. What do you need to stop? What do you need to begin? From whom** do you need to ask forgiveness? To whom do you need to make amends?

The man after God's own heart wanted a clean heart. He no longer denied his sin and its horrible consequences. Neither can we deny that ultimately the heart of David demonstrated itself to be a repentant heart.

In Psalm 51, David expressed more than regret. He desired to change, even to the point of being a teacher of others. His life would be a lesson in holy living.

▶ **22. In order to teach, David needed to be transparent. What keeps a person from admitting his wrong to others?**

_____

_____

_____

How should you respond when someone is transparent regarding the lessons learned in his life?

_____

_____

_____

Is it possible for a person to be too transparent? When?

_____

_____

_____

▶ **23. Read aloud Psalm 51:18–19.**

> In your good pleasure make Zion prosper;
>   build up the walls of Jerusalem.
> Then there will be righteous sacrifices,
>   whole burnt offerings to delight you;
>   then bulls will be offered on your altar.

A Repentant Heart Has a Deep Commitment (vv. 18-19)

Outward acts can give the appearance of inward condition. But David would no longer just go through the motions. He knew that repentance really was an issue of the heart. Sometimes it is easier to make a sacrifice of time or money—but it is always harder when the sacrifice is your own heart.

David's commitment was deep. It was so deep, in fact, that he laid before God his own broken spirit and heart.

The clearest indication that David was different from Saul is his repentant heart. How can you have a repentant heart? Here are five basic principles to follow.

First, do not allow temptation to turn into sin. Temptation per se is not sin. However, any desire that you might have is only one step away from the act. Remember also that Jesus said an intent to sin is as wrong as the act itself. This is what our Lord meant when He said, "'I tell you that anyone who looks at a woman lustfully [a plan to commit sin] has already committed adultery with her in his heart'" (Matt. 5:28).

Second, never cover up or hide sin. This is our first temptation once we fail. It's particularly difficult to admit sin when we know it will lead to embarrassment. However, if we cover our sin, we will not prosper. Furthermore, we are vulnerable to continuing the sin. And as we've seen in David's life, the more he tried to hide the first sin, the more sins he committed. Avoid this predicament by facing the sin immediately and confessing it to God. When necessary, confess it to others you have sinned against. Also, confess it to a trusted friend—someone of the same gender—who can hold you accountable.

Third, acknowledge sin immediately, especially to God. The best way to handle guilt and anxiety is through confession. We must not repress these feelings. If we do, it will eventually lead to self-deception, a hardened heart and a seared conscience.

Fourth, do not take advantage of God's grace. Remember, the Bible says in Romans 1:26 that there comes a time when "God gives man up" to do what he wants to do. Though this is spoken specifically to people who have turned away from God completely, the principle still applies to Christians. When this happens, it is part of God's discipline in our lives. To reap what we sow is sometimes the most painful kind of consequence.

No sin is too great to be forgiven.

Fifth, no matter what the sin and its consequences, confess it and do what is right. The Bible teaches that the blood of Jesus Christ cleanses us from all unrighteousness (1 John 1:9). No sin is too great to be forgiven. We must accept, however, God's forgiveness in Jesus Christ.

At this point, we must follow David's example. After he confessed his sin and received forgiveness, he accepted the consequences of his sin. Scripture says he "got up from the ground . . . washed, put on lotions and changed his clothes." Finally, he "went into the house of the LORD and worshiped" (2 Sam. 12:20).

Do you want to anchor your heart close to God? Have a heart of confession, cleansing, and change. Those are the key ingredients of a repentant heart.

How do you react or respond to the sin in your life? Do you cover up until confronted? Confess your sins whether or not you are confronted. Your heart will not be anchored close to God without confession.

Next, how do you follow up confession? Do you desire cleansing, or do you just want to be "off the hook"? God knows the difference. Your attitude in this affects your closeness to Him.

Man looks on the outward, while God looks on the inside (1 Sam. 16:7). The sacrifices of God are a broken spirit, a broken and contrite heart (Ps. 51:17).

▶ **24. Take a heart exam. Ask God to examine your heart and show you the uncleanness that is there. David's downfall began with a glance. Perhaps God is convicting you of your "glances." Whether they occur on the Internet or in a moment of indiscretion in a crowd, they are wrong. Perhaps a relationship has gone well beyond that and is physical. Adultery is one of the greatest downfalls. In God's view, it is sin. Now is the time to repent. Do not even begin the path that took David to his low point.**

Small-Group Meeting 6

Opening Prayer

Begin your meeting with prayer. Specifically, pray with a repentant heart focused on the subject of sexual immorality. Ask God to help you approach this lesson from David's life with a sensitive heart. Immorality may be a secret sin of someone in your group. Perhaps God will use this lesson to bring about repentance in that person's life. Pray also that there will be seriousness in this study. The world winks at immorality. Ask God to help the group learn that He does not.

Building Relationships

Allow time for each member to share one thing for which they praise God.

Reviewing the Lesson

1. The theme of this lesson is the repentant heart. Have the group review what they learned from the study guide or elsewhere about what repentance means.

2. The story of David and Bathsheba is very familiar, so the review may go quickly. Begin this time by reading the introduction on page 79.

3. Read aloud 2 Samuel 11:1–5. Ask someone to restate in his or her own words what took place in these verses. What were the three ways David tried to cover up his sin?

4. Read aloud Psalm 51, reminding the group that this was written after Nathan confronted David and after he confessed his sin.

5. What are the four characteristics of a repentant heart as found in Psalm 51?

6. What are the five principles of a repentant heart (page 91)?

Applying the Truths to Life

Discussing some of the specific applications of this lesson in a mixed group may be too difficult. You will need to be sensitive as to how open your group can be on this subject. Let members know from the outset that if you feel it is headed in an inappropriate direction or is too explicit, you will stop the discussion and redirect it to an appropriate topic.

Concentrate your discussion on # 8 (page 82) and #13 and #14 (page 85).

Ministering to One Another

One of the ways we can minister to others is to help each live a godly, pure life. Talk about the need to be accountable to one another. Encourage all to develop an accountability relationship.

Reaching Out to Others

Now would be a good time to talk about multiplying by dividing. Perhaps some from your group would take this study material and lead another group through it. Take what you have learned from this experience and share it with others.

Closing Prayer Time

Share prayer requests that have been answered while the group has met and prayed. Spend time praying that God will help each in the group to have a repentant heart. Pray, by God's grace, that each member of the group will be pure sexually.

Notes

Lesson 1

1   For a list of Scriptures to verify the functions of the heart, see Charles F. Pfeiffer et al., eds., *Wycliffe Bible Encyclopedia, Vol. 1* (Chicago: Moody Press, 1975), pp. 767–768.

Lesson 2

1   Davis, Dale. *Looking on the Heart* (Grand Rapids, Mich.: Baker Books, 1994), p. 42.

2   Swindoll, Charles R. *David . . . A Man After God's Own Heart* (*Insight for Living Bible Study Guide,* Waco, Tex.: Word Educational Products Division, nd), p. 25.

3   Ibid.

Lesson 3

1   Alan Redpath, *The Making of a Man of God* (Westwood, N.J.: Fleming H. Revell, 1951), p. 61.

Lesson 4

1   Kenneth L. Chafin, *1 and 2 Samuel* (Dallas: Word Books, 1989), pp. 209–210.

2   Getz, Gene. *David: Seeking God Faithfully* (Nashville, Tenn.: Broadman & Holman Publishers, 1995), p. 114.

3   Swindoll, p. 50.

4   Baldwin, Joyce G. *1 and 2 Samuel: An Introduction and Commentary* (Downers Grove, Ill.: InterVarsity Press, 1988), p. 144.

5   Swindoll, p. 58.

Lesson 5

1   Wiersbe, Warren. *Real Worship* (Nashville, Tenn.: Oliver-Nelson Books, 1986), p. 27.

2   Swindoll, p. 83.

Interacting with God
Small–Group Covenant

Believing that God wants His people to be a healthy Body of Christ with Jesus Christ Himself as its Head, we submit ourselves to Him and to one another so that we may help one another grow into mature believers and so that, as a group, we "may be built up until we all reach unity in the faith and in the knowledge of the Son of God and become mature, attaining to the whole measure of the fullness of Christ" (Eph. 4:12-13). Together we agree to:

1. Study God's Word each week and complete the learning activities for the week's lesson prior to the group meeting.

2. Pray regularly and specifically for one another, our church, our spiritual leaders, and those who need to come into a saving relationship with Jesus Christ.

3. Attend all group meetings unless unavoidable circumstances prevent attendance. If we are unable to attend, we will make every effort to notify our group leader and let him know how the group can pray for us in our absence.

4. Participate in the meetings by listening carefully and sharing openly.

5. Keep confidential any personal matters discussed by other members during the meetings.

6. Seek to demonstrate love as the Holy Spirit leads us to help meet one another's needs.

7. Seek to bring glory and honor to God through our relationships with one another.

Signatures: **Date:** _____

_____   _____

_____   _____

_____   _____

_____   _____

_____   _____

_____   _____

_____   _____

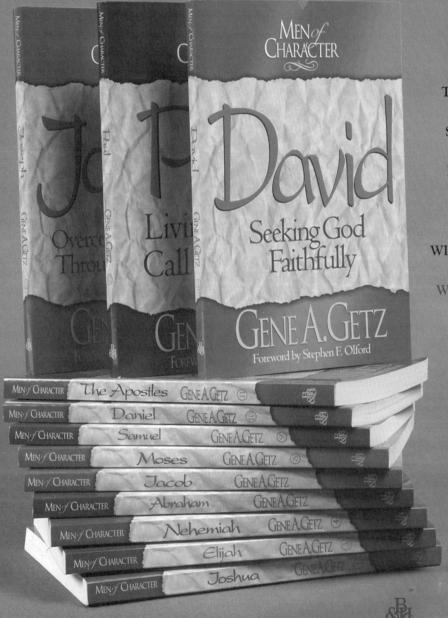